# European Monetary Union

## Lessons from the Classical Gold Standard

M. Panić

*Fellow and Bursar of*
*Selwyn College, Cambridge*

St. Martin's Press

First published in Great Britain 1992 by
THE MACMILLAN PRESS LTD
Houndmills, Basingstoke, Hampshire RG21 2XS
and London
Companies and representatives
throughout the world

Reprinted (with a new preface) 1993

A catalogue record for this book is available from the British Library.

ISBN 0–333–58007–9 hardcover
ISBN 0–333–61184–5 paperback

Printed in Great Britain by
Antony Rowe Ltd
Chippenham, Wiltshire

First published in the United States of America 1992 by
Scholarly and Reference Division,
ST. MARTIN'S PRESS, INC.,
175 Fifth Avenue,
New York, N.Y. 10010

ISBN 0–312–08398–X

Library of Congress Cataloging-in-Publication Data
Panić, M.
European monetary union: lessons from the classical gold standard
/ M. Panić.
p.   cm.
Includes bibliographical references and index.
ISBN 0–312–08398–X
1. Gold standard.   2. European Monetary System (Organization)
I. Title.
HG297.P334   1992
332.4'94—dc20                                        92–4876
                                                          CIP

EUROPEAN MONETARY UNION

*Also by M. Panić*

CAPACITY UTILISATION IN UK MANUFACTURING
INDUSTRY

NATIONAL MANAGEMENT OF THE INTERNATIONAL
ECONOMY

PRODUCT CHANGES IN INDUSTRIAL COUNTRIES' TRADE:
1955–1968 (*with A. H. Rajan*)

UK AND WEST GERMAN MANUFACTURING INDUSTRY
1954–72 (*editor*)

# Contents

v

# List of Tables

# Acknowledgements

This book was made possible by a generous grant from a Sainsbury Family Trust. I am indebted to David Sainsbury, Chairman of John Sainsbury Plc, and his fellow trustees for their support extending over a number of years, as well as for the complete freedom with which I was allowed to pursue my research.

I have also benefited from comments on the manuscript which I received from a number of distinguished economists all of whom have made important contributions in this area of the subject: Professors Arthur Bloomfield, Barry Eichengreen, Alec Ford, Charles P. Kindleberger, David Mayes and Donald Moggridge, and Dr John Wells. I am extremely grateful to all of them. Professor Bloomfield also very kindly allowed me to use some of the data which he had collected for his classic studies of the pre-1914 gold standard.

Finally, I am indebted to three members of the Department of Applied Economics, University of Cambridge, for their help: Diana Day for dealing so promptly and accurately with a large amount of statistical data; Sue Moore who patiently and cheerfully typed more than once the whole manuscript; and Ann Newton who, as usual, read carefully each chapter and suggested stylistic improvements.

M. PANIĆ

# Preface to the Paperback Edition

It is not often that the analysis developed in a book is confirmed by events as rapidly as has been the case here.

The proofs of the text that follows were corrected at the end of March 1992, a few weeks after the publication of the Treaty of Maastricht. By the time the book came out, six months later, the Danes had rejected the Treaty while the French had managed to approve it by the narrowest of margins; and both Italy and the United Kingdom had left the European Exchange Rate Mechanism (ERM) – in each case for reasons considered at some length in this book.

In Denmark and France a high proportion of the voters were concerned about the effects that the centralisation of institutions and harmonisation of policies within the EC might have on the ability of member countries to deal with their national economic and social problems. Italy and the UK, on the other hand, found it impossible to tighten further their already highly restrictive macroeconomic policies. An additional dose of deflation might have kept them within the ERM, but this would have been achieved at the cost of even greater stagnation and unemployment, a trade-off that proved politically unacceptable.

The last two outcomes, in particular, are precisely those predicted in this book. The experience of individual countries under the Classical Gold Standard shows that, no matter how 'irrevocable' its commitments, an independent, sovereign state will break them if the economic and social cost of participating in an international grouping is, or promises to be, against its national interest.

Moreover, although the Danes have approved the Treaty at the second attempt, the worsening economic situation in Europe and its increasingly disagreeable political consequences (especially in Germany) have raised serious doubts about the ability of

EC countries to achieve economic and monetary union by the end of the 1990s. The doubts have become widespread since the speculative attacks on the French franc and other ERM currencies in the summer of 1993 which led to the virtual suspension of the Exchange Rate Mechanism.

The 'convergence criteria' agreed at Maastricht require a country's exchange rate to remain virtually unchanged for at least two years if it is to participate in Stage III of the union. In particular, it must not be allowed to depreciate. In fact, most of the nine countries currently in the ERM have been able to stay within the mechanism over the past year only by devaluing their currencies. The need for frequent realignment of the currencies might be avoided in the future by satisfying the Treaty's fiscal convergence criterion: that public sector deficits should be below 3 per cent and public debt below 60 per cent of the country's GDP. The problem is that, on their past performance, this would have highly adverse effects on output and employment in a number of EC countries, making it inconceivable that they could continue with such policies for long (see W. Buiter, G. Corsetti and N. Roubini 'Excessive Deficits – Sense and Nonsense in the Treaty of Maastricht', *Economic Policy*, April 1993). Consequently, as pointed out in Chapter 5, if EC countries persist with the timetable agreed at Maastricht, a two-tier monetary and economic arrangement in Western Europe seems unavoidable. Convergence of national policies makes sense only if the problems, institutions and policies happen to be very similar.

There is nothing wrong *in principle* with the idea of an international economic and monetary union of the kind that EC countries are trying to create. I show both in this book and elsewhere (Panić, 1988) that, in the long term, the goal represents a logical outcome of the developments and policies that promote international integration and interdependence. However, the viability of such a union depends on the participating countries taking steps to ensure that no member feels that it is worse off within the union than it would have been outside. As comparisons between EC and gold standard countries in the chapters that follow show, that is something that the Community has failed to do; and it is this failure that is at the root of most of its difficulties.

This book is concerned with the basic prerequisites for the creation and viability of an international monetary union and the highly relevant lessons provided in this context by the Classical Gold Standard. The developments of the last two years have not made it necessary to alter either the original analysis or the conclusions, neither of which is affected by them. All that I have done, therefore, is to make a few very small changes in the text. This paperback edition is thus no different from the original version published in September 1992.

CAMBRIDGE, AUGUST 1993                                     M. PANIĆ

# Introduction

The apparent determination of most members of the European Community to create a monetary union by the end of the 1990s has sparked off a heated debate among politicians, bankers, economists and interested laymen. Much of this stems from the fear of influential political groups – particularly strong in the United Kingdom – that the union represents, effectively, the penultimate step in the process of creating a United States of Europe. After all, a monetary and economic union of the kind proposed by the Delors Committee in 1989 and approved by Heads of EC Governments at their meeting in Maastricht two years later requires a common political authority to decide its economic and social priorities.

It is hardly surprising, therefore, that the debate has raised many important questions which, although couched mainly in financial terms, cover much more than the technical aspects of a monetary union. Should member countries be asked to give up their monetary sovereignty? If so, should this be confined to a regime of fixed exchange rates, within the European Exchange Rate Mechanism, or involve something more unifying and finite: a single currency and a single central bank? If the latter, who, in the absence of a common political authority, should be responsible for the Community's monetary policy: the governments of the member countries acting in concert or a politically independent central bank? Finally, if EC monetary integration manages to advance that far, is a monetary union of countries with widely different inflation rates sustainable?

All these are policy issues of considerable practical importance. The problem is that, even when stripped completely of its political undertones, a debate which concentrates on the narrow, financial aspects of monetary unification is unlikely to deal adequately, if at all, with the underlying economic factors that are ultimately responsible for the success and long-term viability of a monetary union.

1

The reason for this is that, paradoxical though it may seem, purely monetary issues constitute the simplest problem to be solved in the formation of an international monetary union. They also happen to be the least important factor in determining its long-term survival.

The main purpose in creating such a union is to facilitate improvements in economic welfare through greater specialisation and trade. This is achieved by eliminating, or at least reducing, all those risks, uncertainties and transaction costs associated with the existence of more than one kind of money. The steps that have to be taken to ensure this are straightforward enough and, as such, have been understood for a long time.

The most effective way of solving the problems created by the existence of two or more monies is, obviously, to replace them with a single common currency – in other words, to form a *complete* monetary union. Alternatively, if they are not prepared to go that far, two or more countries may establish a *quasi* union. All they need to do in this case is to fix their currencies to a common unit of account and thus, by allowing them to be freely convertible into the unit, to each other. They should preferably keep fluctuations in their exchange rates within narrow margins and, at the same time, undertake to maintain the existing parities indefinitely. Provided that these conditions are satisfied, the second arrangement (better known as a regime, or system, of fixed exchange rates) is equivalent to the existence of a single currency with different names in different parts of the union.

The apparent similarities between the two forms that an international monetary union can take are obvious enough. But so are also their differences. To begin with, a single common currency requires a single monetary authority to issue and manage it. That authority may consist either of a single central bank or of several central banks acting in concert under the direction of a single Board of Governors. In contrast, a system of fixed exchange rates allows each country to use its own currency, issued and managed by its own central bank.

Second, the importance of these institutional differences is that they determine the way in which monetary policy is conducted under the two systems: a common policy in the case of complete union and individual national policies when each country retains its own currency. It is easy, however, to exaggerate the importance of this difference, since in practice it turns out to be more apparent than real. The reason for this is that fixed exchange rates cannot be maintained for long if there are significant differences in national monetary policies. When this happens, international capital flows will force the country whose actions are out of step with those of other members of the union either to bring its policy in line with theirs or to leave the union. The smaller the band within which exchange rates are allowed to vary the more illusory will be national monetary independence within a quasi monetary union.

Third, for all these reasons, the difference between the two forms of monetary union that really matters in practice concerns the ease with which a country is able to abandon such an arrangement. As already pointed out, when the single currency model is adopted the responsibility for the monetary policy of the whole union has to be handed over to a supranational institution; and, once this is done, it becomes much more difficult for a country to leave the union than under conditions which allow it to retain its own currency and central bank. In other words, the real freedom in the latter case stems not from a greater ability to pursue an independent monetary policy *within* the union – which is negligible – but rather from a greater ability to *regain* monetary independence by abandoning the union if necessary.

Hence, countries which opt for the 'quasi' (rigidly fixed exchange rates) rather than the 'complete' (single currency) form of monetary union are, in effect, choosing an institutional framework that is relatively easy to dismantle. The motive behind this decision may be either an 'irrational' attachment to their national institutions and currency or a lack of conviction that the collective decision-making process, symbolised by the single central bank, will take into account their specifically national economic problems. Whatever the reason, by choosing the fixed parities version of monetary union, its members are in effect retaining an important policy option: the ability to leave it if greater integration into the international economy, which the union facilitates, works to their disadvantage; and the reasons for this will have little to do with the monetary aspects of the union.

\* \* \*

It follows from what has been said so far that the *creation* of an international monetary union depends on the willingness of independent, sovereign states to give up – either tacitly or openly through a formal agreement – part of their sovereignty; and they will be willing to do so only if membership of the union promises greater *net* economic benefits than those that they could hope to achieve outside it. That being the case, the failure of a monetary union to make its members better off than they would have been otherwise or, equally important, to distribute overall economic gains in a manner which all of them regard as satisfactory, will sooner or later create tensions that will lead to its dissolution. The long-term survival of a monetary union will be determined, therefore, by the success which each member country has in achieving those national economic objectives whose pursuit prompted it to join the union; and this will depend not only on the policies pursued by individual governments but also on compensatory measures which they take collectively to ensure such an outcome in all member countries.

It does not require much reflection to realise that the range and scope of the required measures will vary according to who joins the union. If all the member countries enjoy similar efficiency and income levels, are normally in fundamental equilibrium (in other words, each can reconcile high employment and low inflation levels with a balance on its basic balance of payments) and tend to achieve similar rates of economic growth, few, if any, compensatory measures will be necessary.

By reducing the uncertainties and costs associated with floating exchange rates, a *quasi* monetary union will, as already mentioned, make it easier for its members to improve their economic welfare through greater international specialisation; and their ability to grasp the opportunity with equal success will ensure that they do so to a similar degree. (*Ceteris paribus*, the gains will be even greater under a *complete* monetary union which *eliminates* all these uncertainties and costs.) Moreover, to the extent that regional adjustment problems arise, each country will in this case have the means, as well as the managerial and administrative experience, to deal with them unilaterally, without having to call on the resources and know-how of other members.

In contrast, the further the membership of an international union departs from this ideal the more extensive compensatory measures have to be in order to ensure its long-term survival. Unlike in the previous case, the scale of the problems confronting individual countries will now differ significantly, and the same will be also true of the countries' ability to deal with them. As a result, the period over which the measures need to be implemented will be determined by the length of time that it takes to raise efficiency and income levels in the least prosperous countries of the union to those enjoyed by its most affluent members. The more successful is the union in this respect the more rapidly will it come to resemble the 'ideal' membership described above, making it possible to discontinue gradually most of the compensatory measures.

The factors which determine the ultimate success or failure of a monetary union are too complex to be attributed simply to its existence, even less to its precise monetary arrangements. A complete international monetary union eliminates the problem of balance of payments imbalances within its domain. But it is far from certain that the mere act of creating a single currency and a single central bank will make even a marginal contribution towards removing the existing productivity and income inequalities between regions and countries. In fact, one of the most serious objections to international monetary unions is that they may affect their least prosperous members adversely by making it impossible for them to pursue the macro-economic policies most suited to their needs. Johnson (1972), for instance, used this argument to advocate flexible exchange rates in the belief that they would maintain national economic independence and, thus, the ability of each country to solve its most pressing economic problems.

More pertinently in the present context, Meade (1957), Mundell (1961) and Corden (1972), among others, have argued that a high degree of labour and capital mobility is essential for the success of a monetary union. If this condition cannot be satisfied, the inability of countries to pursue independent macro-economic policies will create serious unemployment problems in the less advanced countries and regions, leading eventually to the union's disintegration.

In other words, implicit in this analysis is the proposition that the larger the disparities in efficiency and income levels the greater has to be the mobility of labour from high unemployment, low wage countries to low unemployment, high wage countries; and vice versa in the case of capital. In theory, other things remaining the same *and* provided that there are no obstacles to this kind of mobility, differences in factor earnings will ensure that they move in such a way as to equalise the productivity and income levels of member countries in the long run.

In fact, the absence of obstacles to international capital and labour movements is no guarantee that they will produce the desired outcome, rather than widen the existing differences. Indeed, the arguments about infant industries (Mill [1848] 1965), cumulative causation (Myrdal 1957), the advantages gained through economies of scale (Krugman 1986) and the known preferences and behaviour of multinationals (Panić 1982, 1991) all suggest that – in the absence of concerted government action, including intergovernmental transfers of resources – further increases in national disparities are the most likely outcome of a monetary union. The larger the differences at the creation of the union the more likely is this to happen. The only way to avoid such a result is for the governments of the most affluent member countries to ensure an adequate transfer of financial and real resources to the least prosperous members in order to assist their long-term development (Panić 1988, EC Commission 1977, Guisinger 1985). It is, of course, far from certain that they will be either willing or able to do this.

For instance, the enthusiasm for joining such a union may subside rapidly in wealthy countries if their populations realise fully the extent to which they will need to finance the adjustment process in members of the union with markedly lower efficiency and income levels. Apart from the fact that this involves higher taxes, which are never popular, there is no guarantee that the less successful countries will have the capacity to undertake fundamental economic and social changes without which a marked improvement in their performance is unlikely whatever the scale of resource transfers from abroad. The less successful countries, normally eager to join a monetary union in the hope that it will assure the sort of transfers that they would not be able to secure otherwise, may also begin to doubt the wisdom of such membership the moment they realise the full scale of the potential costs to them if the transfers fail to materialise. As a result, both groups of countries may become increasingly reluctant to give up formally any aspect of their sovereignty. In such circumstances, those in favour of a monetary union would fail to overcome the first obstacle to achieving their objective.

\* \* \*

This is, probably, one of the reasons why the European Commission has tended to minimise the scale of official resource transfers that may be required to ensure the long-term viability of the proposed economic and monetary union in the European Community (cf. Delors Committee 1989, EC Commission 1990a). For instance, the suggested budgetary transfers are well below those that exist in individual countries – despite the fact that the Commission's own work shows clearly that disparities in efficiency and income levels within the Community are considerably greater than those which exist in industrial countries with federal constitutions such as Germany, the United States, Canada and Switzerland (cf Delors Committee 1989, pp. 84–5; see also EC Commission 1990a, 1990b.)

Considerations of this kind are extremely relevant, since the proposals put forward by the Delors Committee in 1989, and supported by all members of the Community except the United Kingdom, represent the most ambitious effort ever made to create a complex international economic and monetary union while retaining national political institutions and sovereignty.

The transition is to take place in three stages. In Stage One (1 July 1990–31 December 1993) the remaining two members of the European Community, Greece and Portugal, are to join the exchange rate mechanism of the European Monetary System (EMS); and those countries which have still not done so have to liberalise their capital flows completely. Together with the Single Market Act, Stage One is therefore intended to prepare the ground for a complete monetary union in two ways. First, it ensures that capital, like commodities and labour, enjoys total freedom of movement within the EC. Second, it marks the end of 'independent' monetary policies within the Community by fixing all the twelve currencies either within the narrow (± 2.25 per cent) or the wider (± 6 per cent) range of its adjustable peg system. The 'adjustable' aspect of the system indicates that during this stage each member country can still either devalue or revalue its currency relative to the other eleven provided that the latter agree. In other words, Stage One continues the practice, which has characterised the EMS since its inception in 1979, of allowing member countries to realign their currencies.

Stage Two (beginning on 1 January 1994) goes an important step further by transforming the EMS even more firmly into a quasi monetary union. All twelve currencies will have to operate immediately within the narrower (± 2.25 per cent) range and, what is more, will be required to *remain* fixed within it –

though there is a suggestion in the Delors Report that realignments might still be allowed 'in exceptional circumstances' (Delors Committee 1989, p. 38).

However, this particular change is not regarded by the Committee as 'the most important feature of this stage'. It reserves that distinction for its proposal to set up the 'European System of Central Banks'. The 'Eurofed', as the institution has been called, 'would absorb the previously existing institutional arrangements' within the Community, but its 'functions . . . in the formulation and operation of a common monetary policy would gradually evolve as experience was gained' (Delors Committee 1989, p. 38). The Committee suggested that the Bank could be set up in January 1994 – but this view was not shared by, among others, the Bundesbank. The most influential central bank in the Community has insisted that 'the European central bank should not be established until it has been clearly decided which countries are prepared and able, on account of their economic performance, to irrevocably fix the exchange rates of their currencies and to transfer monetary policy responsibility to the Community' (Pohl 1990, p. 10).

The agreement reached by Heads of EC Governments in December 1991 reflects this view. The European Central Bank (ECB) is to be set up by 1 July 1998, or at least six months before a single currency comes into being.

Stage Three is 'to commence with the move to irrevocably locked exchange rates' and by empowering Community institutions to determine overall economic and monetary policies of the Community (Delors Committee 1989, p. 39). Nevertheless, as each country is allowed to retain its currency, transaction costs involved in switching from one currency to another will remain; and the fact that they are allowed to fluctuate ± 2.25 per cent around their par values means that exchange risks will not be completely abolished. Moreover, as mentioned earlier, so long as the countries keep separate currencies and central banks, there is always the possibility that, confronted by serious economic problems, one or more of them might leave the (quasi) monetary union. Stage Three is, therefore, intended to include the ultimate transition: from quasi to a complete monetary union – with national currencies of EC countries which accept this arrangement converted into a single European currency issued by the European Central Bank responsible for the monetary and exchange rate policies of the Community. According to the Treaty of Maastricht, this, final, phase in the creation of the European Monetary Union is to start at the latest on 1 January 1999.

Hence, when the Delors proposals are enacted, the Community countries will move well beyond the arrangements that existed either under the Bretton Woods System (1949–71), which resembled those of Stage One, or under the Classical Gold Standard (1880–1914) which were similar (minus the single central bank and economic union) to those to be introduced under Stage Two and the first phase of Stage Three. In the area of economic policy at least, the Community's institutional framework would essentially be transformed into the kind of system to be found in countries with a federal constitution.

Yet despite the fact that the Community might be subjected to such far-reaching changes, so far the debate stimulated by the Delors Report and the Treaty of Maastricht has concentrated mainly on the two issues – the introduction of a single currency and national monetary sovereignty – in which members of the Community already have much less choice than most governments seem to realise.

The decision to create a single European market – taken in 1987 when all the twelve countries ratified the Single European Act – has, in effect, left the governments little alternative but to create a full monetary union. A single market in goods and factors of production is incompatible with the continuing existence of twelve distinct currencies – each under the control of a separate monetary authority pursuing its own national objectives and policies. The risk that these policies will be incompatible, causing large fluctuations in exchange rates, is sufficiently great to prevent the creation of a *single* market within the Community even if all the administrative barriers to trade and factor movements are abolished.

The choice before EC governments *appears*, therefore, to be straightforward enough: they have either to create a monetary union or abandon the idea of a single European market. In fact, the apparent determination of the twelve governments to create a single market has already given rise at the microeconomic level to developments which are taking the process of European unification, started in the 1950s, to its logical conclusion. Since 1987 many industrial and financial enterprises have spread and rationalised their operations across the Community to an extent that is making the twelve economies even more interdependent than before (cf. Burgenmeier and Mucchielli 1991). As a result, attempts to reverse this process would almost certainly prove to be extremely costly to all concerned; and if this is the case, governments have no realistic alternative but to create a monetary union (Panić 1991).

The most obvious way to do this is to abandon the adjustable peg system, making intra-EC exchange rates unalterable – which is, of course, exactly the suggestion made by the Delors Committee for the early phase of Stage Three, accepted subsequently by EC Governments. However, to be sustained in conditions of completely free capital movements, the quasi monetary union would require member countries to coordinate their monetary policies so closely that they would have no freedom left to take even a moderately independent policy stance. In other words, the loss of monetary sovereignty would be so great in practice that, if they were prepared to accept it, it would be far more rational for them to take the next step and create a full monetary union with a single currency and a single central bank – in other words adopt the second phase of Stage Three. The proposals of the Delors Committee, incorporated in 1991 into the Treaty of Maastricht, represent therefore an attempt to come to terms with the inevitable rather than a hasty, internationalist blueprint for a monetary utopia.

\* \* \*

If the above analysis is correct, it raises a question of fundamental importance: given their apparent differences in efficiency and income levels, what should EC countries do to ensure the long-term viability of their economic and monetary union? After all, a much larger number of countries joined with considerable enthusiasm a quasi monetary union in the late 1920s when they resurrected the classical gold standard. They were convinced that this would make it easier for them to solve their adjustment and stabilisation problems. Yet only a few years later, in 1931, virtually all of them abandoned the standard when confronted with mounting economic problems. Lacking an institutional framework for dealing collectively with a serious crisis, they all tried to solve their own problems in isolation, often at the expense of other countries – despite the fact that this made their economic position even more difficult. The end result was, first, the worst economic slump on record followed, in less than a decade, by the most destructive war in history.

As major differences in productive resources, economic performance and needs were the main reason for the rapid collapse of the interwar gold standard, the question of whether the existing EC disparities – which are far from negligible – present a threat to the viability of the proposed monetary union is therefore of major importance. Unfortunately, it is virtually impossible to answer it unequivocally. A purely theoretical analysis of the issue is bound to be circular: the survival of the union depends on the character and adequacy of the institutional arrangements and policies pursued by the Community; and their feasibility and effectiveness, in turn, will be determined by the size of the existing disparities and the assumptions about behaviour of the countries concerned. Attempts to provide quantitative estimates of the required resource transfers, and the chances that they will be met, are bound to experience similar problems. The answers will inevitably depend on assumptions about 'desired' or 'sustainable' long-term differences in productivity and income levels, and the willingness of the governments and citizens of EC countries to accept them.

An examination of the historical evidence seems, therefore,

a more promising guide to the viability of a European or, for that matter, any other monetary union – providing, of course, that one can find some instance in the past of an international monetary arrangement which was (a) roughly comparable to that contemplated by the EC governments and (b) operated reasonably successfully over a fairly long period. Obviously, this approach cannot be expected to produce a clear-cut answer to the question posed earlier. However, it can, at least, give some idea of the sort of countries capable of forming a monetary union and persevering with it over a long period by actually improving their economic welfare. The existing disparities in the European Community can then be compared to a pattern of international distribution of efficiency and income levels that was apparently 'workable' in the past – remembering, of course, that there are many problems in comparing such data between countries as well as for the same country in different periods.

The nearest example that comes to mind is that of the classical gold standard which operated between about 1880 and 1914. Unlike under the Bretton Woods System (when a country in 'fundamental disequilibrium' was allowed to devalue), countries which tied their currencies to gold were expected to defend the gold parity and thus the exchange rates with other currencies, irrespective of the cost. As a result of this, and given the fact that the currencies were freely convertible and that their exchange rates fluctuated within very narrow margins, those countries that adhered to the standard throughout its existence were, effectively, members of an international monetary union. Moreover, before 1914 there were no restrictions on the movement of capital and labour, and barriers to trade flows were generally much lower than later in the twentieth century. Hence, the gold standard represents a closer parallel to what the EC countries are trying to achieve than does the Bretton Woods System.

One of the dangers of using this particular model for analysing the basic requirements for the success of an international monetary union is that few financial systems, national or international, have been as venerated, vilified and generally misunderstood as the gold standard.

To its admirers, the system which operated in parts of the world for about thirty years before the First World War has come to symbolise a number of enviable qualities: economic progress without inflation; world solidarity (as domestic policy objectives, such as employment, were 'subordinated' to the maintenance of external balances and fixed exchange rates); and proof that sustained improvements in economic welfare could be achieved without the need for governments to overrule the wishes, or interfere with actions, of powerful private interests.

To the critics, on the other hand, the idea that global finances and economic welfare should be determined entirely, or even chiefly, by the availability of a rare metal and the actions of a handful of its producers has always symbolised one of the most absurd policy prescriptions in economics: that nations should sacrifice their economic stability and progress on the altar of what Keynes called 'a barbarous relic'.

Misunderstandings common to both critics and admirers of the gold standard stem from the traditional preoccupation in the literature with a few elementary linkages: the availability of gold, its effect on a country's money supply and the influence of the money supply on economic activity. This ignores the fact that the system which operated from around 1880 until 1914 was both more flexible and far more complex than these grossly oversimplified monetary relationships imply. As will be shown in the chapters that follow, the reasons for the relative success of the gold standard before 1914 can only be understood properly if one takes into account precisely those factors which are normally ignored by monetary economists and historians.

Chapter 1 analyses the origins and the 'rules' of the classical gold standard as well as some of the key characteristics of the countries which observed them throughout the standard's existence. Chapter 2 provides a detailed description of the 'adjustment mechanisms' which are believed to this day to have operated between 1880 and 1914, and the relevant empirical evidence which tells a rather different story. Chapter 3 then examines a number of developments which were responsible for the longevity and apparent success of the gold standard, and the rather special circumstances that made them possible. Chapter 4 brings together the main lessons of the gold standard experience; and Chapter 5 compares disparities in efficiency and income levels between members of the European Community and between a number of countries which were permanent 'members' of the gold standard 'club'.

I hope, therefore, that this short book will be of interest to all those concerned with one of the major economic issues of our time. For whatever happens to the proposals of the Delors Committee, the growing economic interdependence of European and other economies is creating conditions, both in Europe and other parts of the world, which are likely to demand sooner rather than later the formation of at least quasi monetary unions. Although the classical gold standard was primarily a European system, operated by relatively advanced economies, its lessons are of universal importance.

# 1 The Classical Gold Standard: Its Origins, Rules and Domain

There was much less uniformity in monetary and financial arrangements before the First World War than is generally realised. This applies even to the international gold standard which, contrary to widespread belief, never really became a truly global system in the sense that all countries adopted it.

One of the reasons for this was that the arrangements accepted by those who did were not the outcome of a deliberate effort by the international community to promote world specialisation and exchange by agreeing on a uniform code of monetary behaviour. An international conference was held in Paris in 1867 at which most of the participants voted in favour of the gold standard (operated at this time only by the United Kingdom). However, it was not before the mid-to-late 1870s that a number of them actually adopted the standard. Others waited until the 1890s before doing so and quite a few countries either never switched to gold or did so for a short time only.

The international gold standard, therefore, evolved over time – primarily as a result of changes in *national* monetary and financial systems caused by the growing demands made on them in the course of economic development.

## INDUSTRIALISATION AND THE NEED FOR A UNIFORM MONETARY STANDARD

Countries which followed British example and began a sustained process of industrialisation in the early part of the nineteenth century had to overcome, among other difficulties, the constraint imposed on their rate of economic progress by the existence of a rather rudimentary financial framework. There were no banking networks to provide an efficient method of mobilising and allocating savings on a large scale. The existing banks were small and confined to specific localities. Public confidence in their probity and competence was generally low. 'It is safe to say that in the first part of the nineteenth century industrialists only called in the banks when they were absolutely forced to' (Gille 1973, p. 279).

The problem presented by the existence of more than one kind of money and monetary standard was even more serious. A sustained process of industrialisation involves progressively more complex methods of specialisation and, consequently, of interdependence and exchange. The result is a rapid increase in the volume and diversity of economic transactions, a process that cannot advance far without a widely acceptable medium of exchange and – even more important – a single unit of account. The importance of the latter stems from the fact that it is possible for a multitude of transactions to take place using more than one medium of exchange *provided* that there is a single unit of account so that the values (or prices) of goods and services exchanged in different types of money can be compared.

A 'single unit of account' in this context can mean either a single monetary standard or two or more standards whose values are fixed relative to one another. In the latter case, the prevailing system is equivalent to the existence of a single type of money, a single unit of account, with different names. In practice, a single money based on a single standard represents a superior arrangement for the simple reason that it is very difficult to keep the price of different monies fixed in the long term. Actual or expected changes in either demand for or supply of one type of money (or the commodities into which that money is convertible) relative to others will alter its prices in terms of other monies – in other words, its rate of exchange.

Once the prices of different monies start changing, the problem of what constitutes the most appropriate unit of account and the means of deferred payments emerges. It becomes difficult to compare the values of goods and services priced in different types of money; and there is a good deal of uncertainty concerning the most advantageous form of money in which to denominate debts to be settled at some future date. As this is far from easy, the risks involved in trade are considerable. This, in turn, reduces the volume of transactions, diminishing the size of the market for different products and thus levels of specialisation and output. In other words, monetary problems are transmitted to the real side of the economy – retarding the process of economic development.

These were precisely the sort of difficulties encountered in the middle of the nineteenth century in trade between and, often, within national economies. Given the institutional weaknesses mentioned earlier, the only way to overcome the mistrust of money, common to pre-industrial societies, is to base it on a commodity standard. The most obvious candidates for this role, because of their durability, are metals, especially those possessing a high intrinsic value. Gold, silver and to a lesser extent copper satisfy this condition to a degree that cannot easily be matched by other commodities. This explains why they have been used for centuries as money: first as coins and later as the back-up for paper money which could be converted into one or more of them on demand. In the nineteenth century the choice was narrowed down to gold and silver, as copper had dropped out of serious contention during the previous century.

The most serious shortcoming of all commodity standards is that the existing supply tends to be limited by the actual and (in times of crisis) the expected availability of the commodity, while future supply is both erratic and unpredictable (as it depends on new discoveries and/or technical changes in mining and production processes). Hence, expansion of the world economy may be hindered over long periods by shortages of the relevant commodity. Alternatively, the international economy may be subjected to prolonged inflationary tendencies following large increases in its production. Similar swings in national economic activity will be determined by the extent to which a country is capable either of running current account surpluses or of borrowing the relevant commodity, or currencies convertible into it, from other countries.

Not surprisingly, for most of the nineteenth century a country's reliance on gold, silver or both of them depended mainly on which of these metals its residents found easier to acquire, and, as a result, which traditionally formed the largest part of its monetary reserves. Thus by 1870 only the United Kingdom was on the gold standard. Germany, the Netherlands, Scandinavian, Latin American and the major Asian countries were on the silver standard. France, the United States, Belgium, Italy and Switzerland, among others, used both these metals, adhering to a bimetallic standard. Finally, a number of countries – such as Russia, Austria-Hungary and Greece – were forced by wars and revolutions to issue inconvertible paper money (Kenwood and Lougheed 1983, p. 120).

Such a mixture of national monetary systems inevitably created uncertainty concerning the unit of account and the most suitable means of deferred payments internationally and, in some cases, also nationally. In the latter case, the problem was most apparent in the case of countries pursuing bimetallism. In theory, they were less vulnerable to wide oscillations in the price level caused by fluctuations in the quantity of money (brought about either by hoarding or by exports of one of the metals). They also appeared to find it easier to determine and stabilise their exchange rates in a world in which countries were using different monetary standards.

At the same time, the bimetallic standard was potentially highly unstable, posing in countries which adopted it a continuous threat to the unification of their domestic market demanded by sustained economic development. Variations in the supply of gold and silver inevitably affected demand for them, with the result that it was difficult to keep their relative prices fixed. For instance, if the price of silver fell relative to that of gold on international bullion markets, it became profitable to sell the latter abroad for silver. Unless a country's stock of gold happened to be so large that its exports of the commodity restored the relative price of the two metals, or the government intervened to prohibit gold exports, such sales of gold could, in theory, continue until the country ended up with a monometallic (silver) standard.

In other words, there is always a serious risk of instability within integrated, interdependent economic systems using more than one money or monetary standard. For reasons given earlier in this section, the tendency in such a system will be towards a single currency or, if this is not possible, towards its best alternative: different currencies all fixed to the same standard and, therefore, to each other. That is why the argument to the contrary, resurrected recently by Friedman (1990), is anything but convincing. The one historical example that he quotes in support of the virtues of bimetallism – that of France during the first seventy years of the nineteenth century – is so exceptional that it is difficult to regard it as a proof that a bimetallic system need not be unstable. France had unusually large reserves of both gold and silver, a position that cannot be replicated easily. Consequently, all that the French experience illustrates is that, as Irving Fisher pointed out in 1911, '*when conditions are favourable* gold and silver can be kept together for a considerable period by means of bimetallism' (quoted, but ignored, by Friedman 1990, p. 88; emphasis added).

Unfortunately, 'favourable conditions' do not last for ever. The attitude to bimetallism changed significantly in the last quarter of the nineteenth century following a number of important, interrelated developments.

First, discoveries of large new deposits of silver and technical improvements in its production led to a sharp increase in supply, a glut on the world market and a substantial fall in its price relative to that of gold. By the mid 1890s, the market gold–silver price ratio nearly doubled from the level common in the 1870s (Friedman 1990, p. 91). Confronted with the danger of a large increase in the quantity of money and inflation, a number of important countries ceased to coin silver and adopted gold as the sole unit of account. In the process, they dumped on to the market the silver withdrawn from circulation, thus reducing further its price (and attractiveness) relative to that of gold.

Second, the spread of the gold standard after 1870 was made possible by increases in its production during the preceding two decades as a result of new discoveries in Australia and Canada and improvements in mining techniques (see Cooper 1982). The discoveries and improvements enabled national monetary authorities to expand the money supply in response to growing demand brought about by increases in the volume of transactions and wealth, both the outcome of the spread of industrialisation. At the same time, as the rate of increase in gold output declined between the 1850s and the 1890s, the threat of inflation and financial instability appeared to be much less serious under the gold standard than under any alternative regime.

Finally, the fact that the most industrialised country in the world, the United Kingdom, was on the gold standard provided an additional incentive (for those determined to emulate its example) to adopt the same monetary yardstick. To industrialise successfully they had to import a wide range of goods and services from the UK; and given that their export capacity to pay for the required volume of imports was limited, they also needed to raise loans in the City of London, which at the time was by far the most important capital and money market in the world. Thus, adopting the same unit of account as the UK made it easier for those following in its footsteps to expand trade in goods and financial services with 'the workshop of the world'. The attractiveness of a monetary system based on gold increased further in 1873 when Germany, the most important creditor nation after the UK and France, used the indemnity which it had extracted after the Franco-Prussian War to switch from silver to gold.

Two important lessons can be drawn from the triumph of the gold standard in the nineteenth century. First, sustained economic growth, specialisation and exchange are incompatible with a diversity of monetary standards. Sooner or later, the risks and uncertainties that this diversity creates become a serious obstacle to further economic progress. Something has, therefore, to give; and, given the importance which nations attach to their industrial development, it is monetary diversity that will be sacrificed.

Second, much has been made in financial history of the so-called 'Gresham's Law'. The 'law' states that 'bad money' invariably drives 'good money' out of circulation. That may well have been the case in pre-industrial societies relying on metallic forms of money. The inadequate supply and increase in the price of one metal then encouraged people to hoard it, so that the relatively abundant metal ('bad money') became much more important as the medium of exchange. The fact usually overlooked in this analysis is that the change in the use of the two forms of money took place not only because it was profitable but also because the original supply of 'good' coins was inadequate to satisfy the growing demand for money.

However, as the triumph of the gold standard in the nineteenth century shows, provided that the supply of 'good money' is adequate – something that can be easily ensured in systems of inconvertible paper money such as exist today – it is 'good money' that will drive 'bad money' out of circulation. 'Gresham's Law' is, therefore, not only inappropriate but highly misleading as a guide to likely monetary developments in modern industrial economies. A potentially unstable monetary standard, prone to frequent and wide fluctuations, represents as serious an obstacle to economic progress as a diversity of such standards.

It is for this reason that the system adopted by the strongest economy (or economies), with its relatively low rate of inflation and 'strong' currency, will tend to be widely imitated in a world in which levels of international economic integration and interdependence are both high and continuously rising. In other words, it is the monetary standard and practices employed by the dominant economy that will in the end come to dictate national and international monetary arrangements.

## THE RULES

A good deal has been written about the highly demanding nature of 'the rules' that national monetary authorities had to follow under the gold standard. In fact, the rules were no different from those that would have had to be observed under any alternative monetary standard.

To be on a full gold standard *internally*, a country needed to conform to a certain, clearly defined, pattern of behaviour. First, a unit of its currency had to be tied to a specific weight of gold. For instance, the legally specified specie content of the pound sterling was 113 grains of pure gold and that of the US dollar 23.22 grains. Second, it had to permit gold coins to circulate within the economy and its paper money to be fully convertible by the central bank into gold at a fixed price. Third, it had to allow gold to be melted into bullion. Finally, other coins, if used, could play only a subordinate role to gold.

In practice, the laws and regulations required to put these rules into operation varied a good deal from country to country. They also changed over time in individual countries. In the end, according to Bloomfield (1959, p. 14), the United Kingdom and Germany were probably the only countries which strictly observed all the rules, followed closely, at least towards the end of the period, by the United States.

As for other countries, some (including France) were on the so-called 'limping' gold standard. This meant that, legally, their central banks had the option of converting notes into either gold or silver coins. In fact, gold coins were a relatively large part of the currency in circulation in only a few countries (the UK, France, Germany, the United States and, later on, Russia). One of the reasons for this was that in some countries (Austria-Hungary and the Scandinavian countries) people preferred other forms of money. But in several countries which were on the gold standard throughout the period 1880–1914 (Belgium, Switzerland and the Netherlands) central banks were not allowed to exchange notes into gold for the purpose of domestic circulation. Lastly, most of the Scandinavian countries, the Netherlands, Canada and the three important states which adopted the standard only in the late 1890s (Austria-Hungary, Russia and Japan) held their external reserves predominantly in the form of foreign exchange rather than gold. Consequently, in their international financial relations they adhered to the gold *exchange* standard rather than to the gold standard.

The adoption of single monetary standards and single national currencies played an important role in the nineteenth century in the formation of nation states. The creation of a unified monetary and financial system locked different regions of a country into a single economic union depriving them in this way of their economic independence. Regional economies simply became more or less specialised parts of a much larger economic and political entity.

To a certain extent, the spread of the gold standard performed a similar role internationally, at least among the relatively small number of countries undergoing significant and sustained industrialisation. For as soon as these countries adopted gold as the sole unit of account internally they were only a short step away from extending their national monetary systems into a unified *international* gold standard. The step consisted of undertaking to observe two conditions in addition to those described above. To satisfy them, each country had (a) to allow free exports and imports of gold, and (b) to permit non-residents as well as residents to exchange their holdings of its currency either directly into gold or into a currency which was freely convertible into gold.

Once again, however, the fact that the authorities accepted these rules and allowed freedom of international gold movements did not mean that they were indifferent to changes in their monetary reserves, especially in times of crisis. On the contrary, instead of blindly following 'market forces', they frequently took steps, within the limits permitted by 'the rules', to influence the behaviour of the private sector.

For instance, the Bank of France discouraged exports of gold by raising slightly its selling price for gold bars. The same 'gold premium policy' was also employed occasionally after 1890 by the Bank of England (Bloomfield 1959). In addition, the Bank of England and the Reichsbank sometimes raised their buying price of gold, or gave interest free advances to gold importers, in order to encourage inflows of gold. The Swiss National Bank, on the other hand, lowered its gold buying price in 1908 to discourage excessive imports of gold (Bloomfield 1959, p. 53). But this was an exception, as countries on the gold standard were normally concerned with preserving or augmenting their reserves. Switching purchases and sales of gold from the capital to border towns, or the other way round, was another method used by central banks to make gold exports less profitable and imports more so. Some governments (notably those of the Scandinavian countries) floated loans abroad in times of crisis solely for the purpose of obtaining gold and foreign exchange which they then lent to their central banks. Finally, the Reichsbank and the Swedish Riksbank discouraged exports of gold by making it very difficult for commercial banks to obtain it (Bloomfield 1959, p. 54; Fishlow 1985, p. 401).

Nevertheless, the important point about these policies (like those listed earlier in this section) is that they did not alter 'the rules of the game'. They merely introduced a certain degree of flexibility in the way that the gold standard operated – making it more acceptable. In other words, as long as a country adhered to the standard it had no alternative but to observe 'the rules' by pursuing policies that enabled it to remain on the standard. The confident expectation that the most important countries would observe the rules added a degree of credibility to the system (Eichengreen 1992) that has been unique in modern international financial history.

THE EMERGENCE OF AN INTERNATIONAL
MONETARY UNION

The measures described in the previous section, all taken independently by a number of countries, in effect created an international monetary union by either solving automatically or making it easier to solve several problems normally associated with the establishment of a viable international financial system.

The basic problems are:

1. What is to perform the function of money in settling debts between residents of different countries? In other words, what sort of asset is to act as the international medium of exchange, unit of account and store of value?
2. Who is to control the supply of such an asset?
3. As each country has a different kind of money – one of the visible signs of its sovereignty – how are these different currencies to be related to one another?
4. How to make both surplus and deficit countries observe the required stabilisation and adjustment rules? This is essential (a) to avoid hoarding of international liquidity by some countries, causing shortage and loss of liquidity in the rest of the world; and (b) to prevent fluctuations in the value of individual currencies relative to the monetary standard, creating the risks and uncertainties that could destabilise and, if persistent, destroy the system.
5. Who is to act as the lender of last resort, performing a function similar to that discharged at the national level by a country's central bank?

The first problem was solved automatically as all countries which switched to gold operated a common monetary standard. By being the ultimate unit of account, medium of exchange and store of value in each of these countries, gold provided a ready-made asset for settling debts between them – despite the fact that the use of metallic money dwindled into insignificance during the gold standard period.

According to Triffin (1964), in 1815 gold and silver were responsible for two-thirds of the total money supply in the United Kingdom, United States and France. The remaining one-third consisted of credit money (mainly paper money and subsidiary coins) as bank deposits accounted for only 6 per cent of the money in circulation. By 1872, just before the most advanced economies at the time started to adopt the gold standard, there had already been a marked change in these proportions. Credit money accounted now for almost 60 per cent of the total money supply in the three countries, with bank deposits responsible for almost half of this figure. The transformation accelerated over the next forty years, so that in 1913 the share of gold and silver in the total money supply of the gold standard countries was only slightly over 10 per cent. Bank deposits, on the other hand, accounted for almost two thirds of the total. Not surprisingly, it was various credit instruments, such as bills of exchange, that played the key role in settling international debts during the gold standard period. Actual gold transfers were so small that they played directly only a very minor part in international transactions.

These changes in the relative importance of different types of money during the nineteenth century – in both national and international transactions – were the result of two important developments during the period: improvements in the competence, sophistication and innovative capacity of the financial sector in countries undergoing industrialisation; and, as a result, rapidly growing confidence in banks and thus in demand for their services. This, in turn, enabled banks to develop into proper financial intermediaries, spreading their operations both within and between countries.

Nevertheless, although the role of gold in aggregate money supply had shrunk into insignificance, the fact that under the gold standard all forms of money were ultimately convertible into it meant that the metal continued to exercise a dominating influence on total money supply and, through this, an important influence on the volume of transactions within and between countries.

This was possible because the link between the quantity of money in circulation and gold solved also what is invariably a highly controversial problem: who is to be responsible for the creation of international liquidity, and the rules according to which this is to be done? As the currency units of all countries on the gold standard were backed by a clearly specified, fixed, weight of gold, the overall money supply of each country was ultimately determined by its holdings of the metal. The same was true also, of course, of the world economy, or more precisely, of that (very large) part of it which was on the gold standard. The greater the quantity of gold at the countries' disposal the greater was the volume of credit that they could create collectively without causing a crisis of confidence in the whole system and, consequently, the larger was the volume of international transactions that they were able to carry out.

However, in resolving one controversial issue the gold standard created a serious problem of a kind characteristic of all commodity standards. Under the arrangements just described, the overall quantity of gold and, consequently, the global money supply were not determined by the policies of any one central bank or international organisation in line with changes in world output, trade, income and wealth. In the absence of wholesale currency devaluations (in other words, reductions in their gold content) this depended ultimately on new discoveries of gold and/or improvements in mining techniques. Hence, the gold standard ultimately imposed an important constraint on the ability of central banks to increase significantly the quantity of money in circulation in response to long-term economic changes. This would obviously not matter under static conditions. But in a world of rapidly growing economies it is bound sooner or later to undermine the viability of a commodity standard. Although not a serious problem before 1914, this was certainly one of the factors which contributed to the demise of the gold standard after the First World War and a major reason for the subsequent unwillingness of the international community to consider seriously the adoption of a commodity standard.

On the other hand, the adoption of the gold standard by a number of countries automatically solved the third problem mentioned earlier: that of determining the relative values (prices) of national currencies. With each currency unit defined in terms of a clearly specified quantity of gold, the legally determined gold contents of the national currencies established their 'par' exchange rates. Thus, with the pound sterling equivalent to 113 grains of pure gold and the US dollar to 23.22 grains, £1 = $4.87. The par value of currencies was, therefore, equal to their 'mint price' (their gold content).

This does not mean, of course, that under the gold standard exchange rates never diverged from their 'parities'. They did, but not by much. The reason for this was that the margins within which the rates were allowed to float were determined by the cost of transporting gold to another country. For instance, before the First World War the same amount of gold could be bought for £1 in London and for $4.87 in New York so long as the market rate of exchange remained equal to the par value. The problem was that the market rate depended on the demand for and supply of the two currencies. Thus if demand for the dollar increased relative to its supply in London to such an extent that its market rate relative to the pound exceeded the parity by an amount greater than the cost of shipping gold across the Atlantic, it became profitable for those demanding US dollars to export gold to New York and sell it for dollars. Exactly the opposite happened if demand for the pound in New York increased relative to its supply to such an extent that it became more profitable to ship gold to London and sell it for sterling.

The presence of transportation costs obviously meant that market exchange rates could differ from their par values up to the points – the so-called 'gold points' – at which it became profitable to export or import gold. However, the general reduction in transport costs during the gold standard period ensured that these points were quite close, so that in practice exchange rate fluctuations were confined within very narrow limits around their mint parities (cf. Foreman-Peck 1983, p. 71). The exchange rate between the pound and the US dollar, for example, remained for most of the time within the $4.84–$4.90 range. That is, it fluctuated by no more than a little over 0.5 per cent around its par (£1 = $4.87) value.

This unusually (by later experience) rigid adherence to the regime of fixed exchange rates under the classical gold standard was by no means irrational. Despite the considerable improvements mentioned earlier, the sophistication of national financial systems and the extent to which they inspired confidence in both residents and foreigners varied a good deal. In a world of fledgling financial institutions and systems, frequently shaken by scandals and failures, it was risky to put trust in the integrity of banks, including central banks. Their integrity was something that had first to be proved and then carefully maintained. The most convincing proof consisted of a country showing its willingness and, even more important, its ability to accept and observe the gold standard rules described in the previous section. Particularly important in this respect was confidence that the country's central bank would honour the obligation to exchange on demand its currency for gold, or another currency freely convertible into gold, at a fixed price. That depended on the central bank pursuing a monetary policy which ensured that the gold content of its currency remained unchanged. *Ceteris paribus*, so long as it did this, the rate of exchange of its currency into other currencies also remained unchanged.

The rigid maintenance of fixed exchange rates was therefore partly an outcome of the need to generate and sustain confidence in national financial systems. Nevertheless, this particular policy had a very important consequence. With their exchange rates fixed and confidently expected to remain so, all countries which went on gold found themselves effectively on a single currency bearing different names in different countries. In other words, they became members of an international monetary union.

As the remaining two problems that arise in creating an international financial system – those of adjustment and the lender of last resort – will be analysed at some length in the next two chapters, they need be mentioned only briefly here.

The fact that national currencies were tied to gold and freely convertible into it imposed strict stabilisation and adjustment rules on all gold standard countries. There would be an automatic expansion in a country's economic activity if it was earning surpluses on its current balance of payments – and thus receiving gold – *unless* it chose, instead, to lend those surpluses to other countries. For similar reasons, a country running current account deficits – and thus exporting gold – and *unable to borrow* abroad would experience economic contraction. Attempts by surplus countries to deflate or deficit countries to expand their economies would have destroyed the gold standard: surplus countries would have ended up hoarding most of the world's gold while deficit countries would have quickly run down their reserves – making it impossible for them to stay on the standard. (See, however, the next two chapters for an analysis of the way that the adjustment process really worked.)

Finally, no formal attempt was made before 1914 to solve the problem of the international lender of last resort. No international organisation was created to perform this function – which was clearly outside the responsibility of any one national central bank. Nevertheless, they did lend to one another occasionally to avoid serious international financial crises.

'THE CLUB'

An important aspect of the classical gold standard, almost completely ignored in the vast literature on the subject, is the fact that it operated continuously between 1880 and 1914 only in a relatively small number of economies.

Some countries – including both very large and fairly large ones such as China, Brazil and Spain – never adopted the gold standard. Some (Argentina, Italy, Mexico, Portugal and Bulgaria) did so for a short time, abandoned it and then, in a few cases (Argentina, Italy and Bulgaria), re-adopted the standard later either legally or *de facto*. Even the United States, which during this period became the most industrialised country in the world, kept its options open until 1900. For it was only then that it legally abandoned bimetallism, though it had been on the gold standard *de facto* since 1879. Finally, a number of important countries (Austria-Hungary, Russia and Japan) joined the gold standard system in the 1890s, after it had been in operation for almost twenty years. Consequently, only relatively few nations were able to stay on the gold standard throughout the thirty odd years of its existence, forming a rather exclusive 'club'. But there was nothing accidental about this exclusiveness. As Tables 1.1 and 1.2 show, with one or two exceptions, the members were rather different from the rest of the world. To begin with, Canada apart, countries in Group A ('The Club') had begun the process of sustained economic development earlier than those in Group B. This means that members of 'The Club' adopted the gold standard only some time after completing the initial stage of industrial development, something that was also true of a number of latecomers (Austria-Hungary, Russia and Japan).

The sequence is important for two reasons. First, industrialisation requires a reasonably orderly and effective financial system – a precondition also for being able to observe the short-term stabilisation rules demanded by an international monetary union. Second, countries with a successful record, or prospects of industrial development normally find it easier to attract the foreign capital without which it would be virtually impossible for them to finance their import requirements and, thus, to maintain a particular exchange rate over a long period without serious losses in economic welfare. Among the countries included in Table 1.1 which adopted the gold standard *before* the start of sustained economic development, only Canada was able to maintain the gold parity throughout the period.

Not surprisingly, Table 1.2 shows that the difference between Groups A and B in per capita levels of industrialisation (measured as the volume of manufacturing output per head) and income was considerable. (It would be even more pronounced if the data for Austria-Hungary referred to the whole empire rather than to Austria, its most advanced part.) What is

Table 1.1  Per capita levels of GNP and industrialisation under the classical gold standard, 1880–1914: selected countries

| | Approximate date of adopting gold standard | Approximate date of the beginning of sustained economic growth | Per capita levels of industrialisation[a] (UK 1900 = 100) | | Per capita GNP levels (1960 $US and prices) | |
|---|---|---|---|---|---|---|
| | | | 1880 | 1913 | 1880 | 1913 |
| *Group A: Permanent members* | | | | | | |
| UK | 1821 | 1780s | 87 | 115 | 731 | 1 070 |
| Canada | 1867 | 1890s | 10 | 46 | 632 | 1 110 |
| Germany | 1873 | 1850s | 25 | 85 | 432 | 775 |
| Sweden | 1874 | 1860s | 24 | 67 | 404 | 705 |
| Norway | 1874 | 1860s | 16 | 31 | 376 | 615 |
| Denmark | 1874 | 1860s | 12 | 33 | 431 | 885 |
| Netherlands | 1874 | 1850s | 14 | 28 | 492 | 740 |
| Finland | 1874 | 1860s | 15 | 21 | 332 | 525 |
| France | 1878 | 1830s | 28 | 59 | 483 | 670 |
| Switzerland | 1878 | 1850s | 39 | 87 | 584 | 895 |
| Belgium | 1878 | 1820s | 43 | 88 | 481 | 815 |
| USA | 1879 | 1840s | 38 | 126 | 794 | 1 350 |
| *Group B: Latecomers, stragglers and outsiders* | | | | | | |
| Austria-Hungary | 1892 | 1870s | 15 | 32 | 427[b] | 700[b] |
| Russia | 1897 | 1890s | 10 | 20 | 252 | 345 |

| | | | | | | |
|---|---|---|---|---|---|---|
| Japan | 1897 | 1880s | 9 | 20 | 201 | 310 |
| Italy | 1878, 1902 | 1890s | 12 | 26 | 289 | 445 |
| Argentina | 1881, 1900 | 1930s | n.a. | n.a. | n.a. | 401 |
| Bulgaria | 1899, 1906 | n.a. | 6 | 10 | 215 | 285 |
| Mexico | 1900–10 | 1940s | 4 | 7 | n.a. | 165 |
| Portugal | 1890$^c$ | n.a. | 10 | 14 | 285 | 335 |
| Spain | – | n.a. | 14 | 22 | 304 | 400 |
| Brazil | – | 1930s | 4 | 7 | n.a. | 186 |
| China | – | 1950s | 4 | 3 | 192 | 188 |
| WORLD | – | – | 9 | 21 | 250 | 364 |

[a]Three-year averages. [b]Austria only. [c]Left the gold standard. n.a. = not available

*Souces*: Gold standard dates – Kenwood and Lougheed (1983) and Bloomfield (1959). Dates for the beginning of sustained economic development: Rostow (1978 and 1980). Per capita levels of industrialisation: Bairoch (1982). GNP per capita: 1913 – Bairoch (1981); 1880 – rates of change between 1860 and 1880 in Bairoch (1976) applied to Bairoch's estimates for 1860 (Bairoch 1981). The US rate of change taken from Rostow (1980); and the Canadian figure for 1880 (Rostow 1980) and Brazil's for 1913 (Maddison 1989) were scaled to the US estimates for 1880 and 1913 respectively given in this table.

*Table* 1.2　Differences in per capita levels of industrialisation and GNP in 1880 and 1913

| | Industrialisation (UK 1900 = 100) | | GNP (1960 $US and prices) | |
|---|---|---|---|---|
| | 1880 | 1913 | 1880 | 1913 |
| **Group A** | | | | |
| Mean | 29 | 66 | 514 | 846 |
| Coefficient of variation (%) | 72.4 | 53.0 | 27.8 | 27.6 |
| **Group B** | | | | |
| Mean | 9 | 16 | 271 | 342 |
| Coefficient of variation (%) | 44.4 | 56.2 | 28.0 | 44.2 |
| *Ratio of the mean levels* | | | | |
| A/B | 3.22 | 4.12 | 1.90 | 2.47 |
| ***************** | | | | |
| **Group A (Bottom 5 countries[a])** | | | | |
| Mean | 18 | 41 | 395 | 651 |
| Coefficient of variation (%) | 33.3 | 48.8 | 10.6 | 12.9 |
| **Group B (Top 5 countries[b])** | | | | |
| Mean | 12 | 24 | 295 | 440 |
| Coefficient of variation (%) | 16.7 | 20.8 | 28.5 | 35.0 |
| *Ratio of the mean levels* | | | | |
| A/B | 1.50 | 1.71 | 1.34 | 1.48 |

[a]1880: Finland, Norway, Sweden, Denmark and Germany. 1913: Finland, Norway, France, Sweden and the Netherlands. [b]Austria-Hungary, Italy, Spain, Russia and Japan.
*Source*: Calculated from Table 1.1.

more, the difference widened between 1880 and 1913, as both industrialisation and productivity and income levels increased faster in the more advanced group. The widening of the gap was accompanied by marked changes within each group. In Group A the dispersion in per capita income remained unchanged, but there was a clear narrowing of differences in per capita levels of industrialisation. In contrast, the dispersion in Group B increased – as some countries began to industrialise at the turn of the century while others were to do so only decades later.

As a result, far from being a world-wide monetary system, the classical gold standard was basically confined to the most advanced economies at that time. Only they could observe for more than a third of a century the very strict and demanding rules of an international monetary union, dictated by its most advanced economy, that of the United Kingdom, without any detrimental effects. In fact, as will be shown in the next two chapters, far from experiencing any such effects, each member of 'The Club' improved its economic welfare, in a number of cases dramatically so. Lack of comparable data has made it necessary to restrict the coverage in Table 1.1 to twenty-three countries. However, on the basis of the economic histories and known achievements both of these countries and of the countries left out, there is no reason to doubt the validity of this conclusion.

## CONCLUSIONS

The triumph of the gold standard among the more advanced economies in the last quarter of the nineteenth century owed a good deal to two factors: the difficulty of achieving greater national and international division of labour without a single unit of account; and the fact that this was the standard that had been adopted more than half a century earlier by the UK, the world's most industrialised nation – providing by far the largest share of international capital, manufactured goods and the know-how essential for the industrialisation of other countries. Once on the standard, members of 'The Club' were able to overcome a number of the difficulties which even to this day have presented a major obstacle to the creation of a viable, lasting international monetary system.

The decision to take the steps which, in effect, amounted to joining an international monetary union was made easier by the absence of formal treaties which required the countries to 'harmonise' their economic policies, or to adopt the standard by a certain date. In fact, considerable differences remained in the way that they pursued their economic – even monetary – policies. Even more important, sovereign nation states adopted the standard when they were in a position to follow the rules and felt sure that this would be in their national interest. If it was not, the decision to switch to gold was far from irrevocable: they could, and quite a few did, leave the standard. Some of them abandoned it for ever, others to rejoin it at a later date when they could accept the rules without having to sacrifice their domestic economic and political objectives.

# 2 How the Classical Gold Standard Did Not Work

Research over the last thirty years has done a good deal to destroy many of the myths surrounding the classical gold standard. For instance, it is clear from the historical evidence included in the previous chapter that the standard was by no means a truly global monetary system. A number of large, or fairly large, countries never tied their currencies to gold; and some of those that adopted the practice did not hesitate to abandon it when the cost of observing 'the rules' became too great. This tended to confine membership of 'The Club' to the most advanced economies of the time. Moreover, although a number of countries made great strides in industrialising their economies, the rates of growth achieved between 1880 and 1914 were neither as high nor as stable as after the Second World War (Maddison 1982, Boltho 1989).

Nevertheless, one myth has remained virtually intact: the belief that the classical gold standard 'worked' because, unlike in the interwar period, the countries that adopted it did not hesitate to sacrifice employment and income in order to eliminate deficits on their *current* balances of payments – thus ensuring that the currencies remained fixed to gold and to each other (cf. Eichengreen 1985, p. 24). As a result, the adjustment process is still believed to have operated automatically, quickly producing the desired outcome (Ford 1989).

In reality, as will be shown in this chapter, no member of 'The Club' was put in a position in which it had to sacrifice its economic welfare for the sake of maintaining external balance. Contrary to the conventional wisdom, some of the most impressive increases in output and income between 1880 and 1914 were achieved by countries running virtually persistent trade deficits.

## THE CLASSICAL/NEOCLASSICAL ADJUSTMENT PROCESS IN THEORY

The standard description of how the balance of payments adjustment process is supposed to have worked when currencies were rigidly tied to gold is provided by the price-specie flow 'mechanism' developed in the middle of the eighteenth century by David Hume, the Scottish philosopher (Hume [1752] 1985), and elaborated subsequently by a number of economists, notably J. S. Mill ([1848] 1965).

The 'mechanism' has three important features. First, it operates in a world in which only goods are traded internationally. Factors of production, while perfectly mobile within countries, are completely immobile between them. This means that trade deficits have to be eliminated promptly since no country is capable of financing them for long out of its own reserves.

Second, the process by which the deficits are removed is entirely automatic. It requires, therefore, no 'interference' from governments and central banks. This is made possible by a number of important assumptions about the world in which the price-specie flow model operates. To begin with, there is no technical change and no economic growth. It is also a world of perfect competition in factor and commodity markets. Both wages and prices are perfectly flexible, ensuring that there is always full employment. Money is demanded for transaction purposes only. It consists entirely of gold coins and notes freely convertible into gold by both residents and non-residents. As the quantity of a country's currency in circulation is rigidly fixed to a clearly specified weight of gold (and thus to other currencies on the standard) its money supply is determined by the amount of gold at its disposal.

The absence of innovative activity extends to the world of finance where the institutional framework is rudimentary and remains so. The same applies also, of course, to the means for settling debts both nationally and internationally. As there are no capital flows between countries, external deficits have to be financed by exporting gold (the only asset used for this purpose) from deficit to surplus economies. The shipment of gold alters the quantity of money in circulation in all members of the system.

Finally, the automatic nature of the processes set in motion by trade imbalances and the movement of gold ensures that the operation of the price-specie flow mechanism is perfectly symmetrical. In other words, what happens in a country experiencing current account deficits and losing gold is exactly the reverse of developments in a country enjoying current account surpluses and thus accumulating gold. Consequently, either of these cases is sufficient to give a full account of the adjustment process that follows. However, as under fixed exchange rates the urgency to undertake external adjustment (and the resistance to it!) generally tends to be much greater in deficit than in surplus countries, this section will concentrate on the kind of changes taking place in a deficit country.

Suppose, for instance, that a country is in fundamental equilibrium – enjoying full employment, price stability and balance on its trade in goods and services (Panić 1988, chapter 3). Then something happens to disturb the equilibrium: a natural disaster, a bad harvest, or war – supply shocks which diminish the country's supply of goods and services relative to demand. As a result, prices go up. With prices in the rest of the world remaining unchanged, there is an increase in imports while exports decline (partly because they are more expensive and partly because it is now more profitable to sell these products on the home market). The balance of payments turns into deficit, financed by exports of gold.

The loss of gold causes the quantity of money in circulation to contract; and the strict legal requirement for coins to contain, and notes to be convertible on demand into a clearly specified amount of gold prevents the central bank from issuing more coins and notes to keep the supply of money unchanged. In jargon, it is not able to 'sterilise' the outflows.

As money is held for transaction purposes only, the fall in its quantity leads automatically to a contraction in aggregate demand and output. Excess capacity and unemployment bring money wages and prices down, stimulating external demand for the country's exports while its own demand for imports falls. The changes eliminate the current account deficit, enabling the country to reconcile its internal and external balances. However, the equilibrium has been restored through a fall in the standard of living (real wages). Without this, domestic demand would not have contracted sufficiently to ensure the required increase in exports and reduction in imports.

The adjustment process described so far can be summarised in a way which makes it easier to follow the sequence predicted by the price-specie flow model:

$$\downarrow \ bp = f(p) \qquad \uparrow \qquad\qquad (1)$$

$$\downarrow \ m = f(bp) \qquad \downarrow \qquad\qquad (2)$$

$$\downarrow \ y = f(m) \qquad \downarrow \qquad\qquad (3)$$

$$\downarrow \ w = f(y) \qquad \downarrow \qquad\qquad (4)$$

$$\downarrow \ p = f(w) \qquad \downarrow \qquad\qquad (5)$$

$$\uparrow \ bp = f(p) \qquad \downarrow \qquad\qquad (6)$$

where *changes* in the key variables are indicated by: $bp$ = current balance of payments; $p$ = prices; $m$ = money supply; $y$ = output and $w$ = money wages. The arrows show the expected direction of change in a variable, in other words whether it is expected to increase or decrease.

A country experiencing a fall in prices, a trade surplus and gold imports would, of course, go through exactly the reverse process. Consequently, it is impossible to have persistent deficits in some countries and surpluses in others. Whatever the disturbance, it is assumed to give immediate rise to changes in relative prices followed by gold movements that will quickly restore the whole system to equilibrium.

Implicit in the preceding analysis is an important advantage enjoyed by countries on the gold standard: the fact that the same asset, gold, is used to settle debts both within and between countries. Hence, although a disturbance of the kind described earlier will reduce real wages in a deficit country, the change need not be abrupt. The reason for this is that its residents can use the gold circulating as money within the country to purchase foreign products and thus temporarily ease the impact of, say, a bad harvest on their standard of living. By contrast, if international exchange consisted entirely of barter, or if international payments were made in an asset which was not as readily acceptable as gold, this particular country would have experienced widespread starvation and loss of population.

The ability to finance an unanticipated external deficit will be ever greater if countries keep some of their gold and foreign exchange (convertible into gold) in reserve for precisely such a contingency. In this case, Hume's position of $X - M = 0$ (where $X$ and $M$ represent, respectively, exports and imports of goods and services) can be modified into $X - M - G = 0$ (where $G$ indicates movements of gold and foreign exchange). Obviously, the larger $G$ is the easier it is to delay the full impact of a trade deficit on the standard of living. But the adjustment process described earlier cannot be postponed for long. Countries have only very limited reserves of gold; and $G$ does not alter either the kind of economic problems confronting those running external deficits or the reaction of their economic agents to these problems. Consequently, *ceteris paribus*, $G$ cannot stop the original disturbances from sooner or later setting into motion the sequence of events predicted by Hume.

This remains true even if the price-specie flow model is made more realistic by incorporating into it the interest rate 'mechanism'. Changes in the money supply relative to the demand for money are bound to affect the rate of interest; and, in the absence of exchange controls, changes in a country's interest rates relative to those of other countries will give rise to short-term accommodating capital flows when nations trade in financial assets as well as in goods (see Whale 1937). Not surprisingly, the importance of interest rates and short-term capital flows was recognised fairly early in the history of the gold standard (cf. Goschen [1861] 1890). This means that, thanks to arbitrage in international money markets, a current account deficit can be financed for a time not only by $G$ but also by inflows of $STC$ (short-term capital): $X - M + STC - G = 0$.

In the classical/neoclassical model the interest rate mechanism is as effective in financing temporary disequilibria as the price-specie flow mechanism is in eliminating them. With the exchange rates of the gold standard countries fixed and confidently expected to remain indefinitely at the existing parities – and no exchange controls – the market for financial assets, like other markets, is assumed to be perfectly competitive. This means that short-term international capital flows are highly responsive to relative changes in interest rates; and these are, of course, triggered off by changes in a country's monetary condition relative to those prevailing in the rest of the world. As pointed out earlier, with monetary conditions influenced by external disequilibria, it is quite easy to integrate short-term financial flows and interest rates into the Hume model without changing its basic characteristics.

To illustrate this, suppose again that there is an unanticipated current account deficit. This reduces the quantity of money in circulation and, in the process, raises interest rates relative to those in other countries. Relatively higher interest rates imply relatively lower bond prices (as residents sell bonds to replenish their stock of money), making it profitable for non-residents to acquire the country's securities. As a result, short-term funds flow in, preventing the quantity of money from declining as rapidly as it would have done in their absence. If domestic and foreign assets are perfect substitutes, short-term funds will flow in until the country's asset prices and interest rates become equal to those prevailing abroad; and, so long as the inflows take place, the country will acquire an additional stock of foreign currencies and gold with which to finance its current account deficit.

What happens to this deficit will depend on the nature of the original disturbance and the way that the 'real' side of the economy responds to higher interest rates – in other words, on the interest rate elasticity of demand for goods. If, as assumed by classical and neo-classical economists, it is high – a rise in interest rates will intensify the deflationary pressure on the economy by increasing the cost of borrowing. Despite the ability to acquire short-term funds from abroad, this should lead to a speedy elimination of the external imbalance along the lines described by the original model. The fall in output, wages and prices will correct the balance of payment (equations 4–6), reconciling internal and external balances. Moreover, lower output and income will reduce the demand for money and, with it, interest rates – raising the price of domestic financial assets to that of their foreign equivalents. Thus equilibrium is restored in commodity, factor and asset markets.

Exactly the same thing will happen also, though by a slightly different route, if the interest rate elasticity of demand for goods is low. In this case, by boosting domestic money supply, inflows of short-term capital from abroad will reduce the fall in aggregate demand, output, prices and wages below what it would have been otherwise. However, in doing this, the inflows will also delay the return to a current account balance; and it is the persistence of this imbalance that triggers off external pressure for adjustment.

The reason for this is that the longer the deficit persists the higher will domestic interest rates have to rise in order to compensate for the growing risk that the country will be unable to sustain the existing exchange rate. As a result, sooner or later the risk premium involved in buying assets denominated in the country's currency will rise sharply. When this happens, the adjustment process will be set in motion either because the flow of short-term funds will be reversed or because domestic interest rates will rise to prohibitive levels, choking off aggregate demand despite its low interest rate elasticity.

These developments will ensure that, as before, all three markets (for commodities, factors and assets) return to equilibrium. Moreover, given the assumption of perfect international arbitrage, the delay in the adjustment process is not likely to be great. Free international trade and capital movements, combined with perfect information, will ensure that domestic prices and interest rates are quickly brought into line with those in other countries.

Either way, the predictive sequence of the adjustment process in the model which includes short-term capital flows is not fundamentally different from that described earlier:

$$\downarrow \quad bp = f(p) \quad \uparrow \tag{7}$$

$$\downarrow \quad m = f(bp) \quad \downarrow \tag{8}$$

$$\uparrow \quad i = f(m) \quad \downarrow \tag{9}$$

$$\uparrow \quad stc = f(i) \quad \uparrow \tag{10}$$

$$\downarrow \quad m = f(stc) \quad \uparrow \tag{11}$$

$$\downarrow \quad y = f(m) \quad \downarrow \tag{12}$$

$$\downarrow \quad w = f(y) \quad \downarrow \tag{13}$$

$$\downarrow \quad p = f(w) \quad \downarrow \tag{14}$$

$$\uparrow \quad bp = f(p) \quad \downarrow \tag{15}$$

where $stc$ = changes in short-term capital movements, $i$ = changes in interest rates and *broken* arrows show that changes in the indicated direction are taking place more slowly than would have happened in the absence of $stc$.

In conclusion, the classical/neoclassical model of the adjustment process under the gold standard has proved to be remarkably durable and highly influential. Almost two centuries after Hume no lesser an authority than Jacob Viner (1937, p. 291) wrote that: 'The "classical" theory of the mechanism of international trade, as developed from Hume to J. S. Mill, is still, in its general lines, the predominant theory. No strikingly different mechanism has yet been convincingly suggested. . . .' That may well have been true in the mid 1930s, but did the durability and reputation of 'the mechanism' rest on firm empirical foundations? After all, the relevance of a theoretical model in economics depends on its ability to explain accurately a particular aspect of human behaviour, making it possible to predict correctly (a) the most likely outcome of certain events and (b) the consequences of alternative policy options available to deal with them.

The classical/neoclassical model of the adjustment process under the gold standard contains three important predictions. First, current account imbalances (both deficits and surpluses) cannot last long because changes in monetary conditions and prices, which they trigger, will set in motion the adjustment process and thus restore equilibrium. Second, the adjustment process will reduce real income in deficit countries and raise it in surplus ones. The loss of economic welfare in the former will be either absolute or relative, depending on whether the existing economic conditions (national and international) are static or dynamic. Lastly, economic developments taking place in surplus countries will be exactly the opposite of those in economies experiencing external deficits. This means, for example, that levels of exports, money supply, output and wages will go up in surplus countries and decline in deficit ones. The latter, on the other hand, should experience higher levels of prices, imports, interest rates and short-term capital inflows – all of which will, of course, be reduced in surplus countries. Under dynamic conditions, the model implies that the first group of variables will grow faster in surplus countries and the second group in deficit ones. Is this what actually happened to countries which were on the gold standard between 1880 and 1914?

THE EVIDENCE: THE ADJUSTMENT PROCESS

The accuracy of the 'mechanisms' described in the previous section has been questioned by many writers – invariably in relation to a particular aspect in which the available evidence showed the experience of one or more countries to have differed from the theoretical predictions (Williams 1920, Viner 1924, Taussig 1927, White 1933, Cassel 1935, Bloomfield 1959, Ford 1962, Triffin 1968, McCloskey and Zecher 1984). However, the 'partial' nature of the analyses made it very difficult to question the validity of the price-specie flow model as a whole, especially when applied to members of the 'The Club'. One is left therefore with the impression that, although not perfect in every respect, the adjustment process was indeed as automatic and efficient as portrayed in the model developed by classical and neoclassical economists.

The problem is that the more one examines the large volume of statistical data collected in recent decades by economic historians the more difficult it becomes to subscribe to the traditional view that the gold standard worked because the countries concerned were prepared to sacrifice their economic welfare in order to observe the financial discipline imposed on them by membership of an international monetary union.

The reason for this emerges clearly from an analysis of the experience of seven countries for which virtually all the relevant data are available. Six of them were permanent members of the 'The Club'. Of these, the three Scandinavian countries had in the 1870s formed a monetary union of their own based on a common currency, the Scandinavian krona (Jonung 1984). The seventh country, Italy, is interesting because, as pointed out in the previous chapter, it first left the standard for slightly over a decade (between 1891 and 1902) and then rejoined it informally until its end.

Although the sample is small, the data set out in Tables 2.1–2.3 indicate that it consists of three distinct groups of economies. To begin with, contrary to the predictions of the price-specie flow model, the United Kingdom and Germany earned current account surpluses in every single year between 1880 and 1914. What is more, the surpluses were far from negligible. In the UK's case they averaged around 4.5 per cent of the country's GDP at current prices, varying from as low as 0.9 per cent in 1901 to as high as 8.9 per cent in 1913. The German surpluses were more modest relative to GDP: an average of 1.8 per cent, with the lowest surplus 0.4 per cent (1907) and the highest 3.4 per cent (1905). However, it is clear from Table 2.3 that the observed differences between the highest and the lowest figures were rather exceptional, as fluctuations around the mean tended to be small in both countries.

Table 2.1  Some gold standard 'inconsistencies', 1880–1913
(number of years)

| | Current balances of payments | | Money supply | | Central bank discount rates | | GDP | | Nominal wages (industry) | | Real wages (industry) | | Consumer prices | |
|---|---|---|---|---|---|---|---|---|---|---|---|---|---|---|
| | S | D | I | F | I | F | I | F | I | F | I | F | I | F |
| UK | 34 | 0 | 26 (2) | 6 | 19 | 14 | 26 (3) | 5 | 17 (7) | 10 | 20 (2) | 12 | 15 (7) | 12 |
| Germany | 34 | 0 | 28 | 6 | 21 | 12 | 31 | 3 | 24 (7) | 3 | 24 (1) | 9 | 20 (1) | 13 |
| Italy | 24 | 10 | 27 | 7 | n.a. | | 25 | 9 | 13 (19) | 2 | 23 (1) | 10 | 18 (2) | 14 |
| USA | 18 | 16 | 30 | 4 | n.a. | | 29 | 5 | 28 (3) | 3 | 28 (1) | 5 | 7 (22) | 5 |
| Norway | 10 | 24 | 29 (1) | 4 | 14 (6) | 13 | 30 | 4 | n.a. | | n.a. | | 19 (3) | 12 |
| Sweden | 7 | 27 | 34 | 0 | 13 (6) | 14 | 31 (1) | 2 | 29 (4) | 1 | 27 | 7 | 19 | 15 |
| Denmark | 2 | 32 | 26 (2) | 4 | 15 (4) | 14 | 33 (1) | 0 | n.a. | | n.a. | | 15 | 19 |

S = surplus. D = deficit. I = increase. F = decrease. Figures in brackets = no change. n.a. = not available.
*Sources*: GDP and consumer prices – Maddison (1982). Current balances of payments, money supply (except for Italy) and wages – Mitchell (1975 and 1983). Italian money supply – Fratianni and Spinelli (1984). Central bank discount rates – data supplied by Arthur I. Bloomfield.

Table 2.2 Current account balances and economic development under the classical gold standard (average annual percentage changes[a])

| | Current balance as % of GDP | Money supply | Central bank discount rates (%) | GDP | Nominal wages | | Consumer prices | Real wages | |
|---|---|---|---|---|---|---|---|---|---|
| | | | | | Industry | Agriculture | | Industry | Agriculture |
| **1880–1913** | | | | | | | | | |
| **WORLD** | | | | 2.9 | | | 0.2[b] 0.1[c] | | |
| UK | 4.5 | 2.0 | 3.5 | 2.0 | 0.8 | 0.4[d] | 0.1 | 0.7 | 0.8[d] |
| Germany | 1.8 | 6.5 | 4.1 | 3.0 | 1.9 | 1.6 | 0.7 | 1.3 | 0.9 |
| USA | 0.7 | 5.6 | n.a. | 4.2 | 1.8 | n.a. | 0.2 | 1.7 | n.a. |
| Italy | 0.6 | 3.3 | n.a. | 1.8 | 1.7 | n.a. | 0.6 | 1.2 | n.a. |
| Sweden | -2.5 | 5.4 | 4.7 | 2.8 | 2.7 | 2.7 | 0.5 | 2.1 | 2.1 |
| Norway | -2.5 | 5.9 | 4.7 | 2.2 | n.a. | n.a. | 0.5 | n.a. | n.a. |
| Denmark | -2.6 | 2.6 | 4.3 | 2.9 | n.a. | n.a. | -0.1 | n.a. | n.a. |
| **1880–1896** | | | | | | | | | |
| **WORLD** | | | | 2.6 | | | -1.6[b] -1.0[c] | | |
| UK | 4.5 | 2.2 | 3.4 | 2.3 | 0.5 | 0.6 | -1.1 | 1.6 | 1.2 |
| Germany | 2.1 | 5.3 | 3.6 | 2.8 | 1.4 | 0.6 | -0.5 | 1.5 | 0.7 |
| USA | -0.6 | 4.8 | n.a. | 3.8 | 1.6 | n.a. | -0.6 | 2.3 | n.a. |
| Italy | -0.3 | 1.6 | n.a. | 0.7 | 1.0 | n.a. | -0.1 | 1.4 | n.a. |
| Sweden | -2.9 | 3.6 | 4.2 | 2.2 | 2.1 | 1.9 | -0.5 | 2.5 | 2.4 |
| Norway | -0.4 | 4.3 | 4.3 | 1.7 | n.a. | n.a. | -0.8 | n.a. | n.a. |
| Denmark | -1.9 | 1.1 | 3.6 | 2.6 | n.a. | n.a. | -0.9 | n.a. | n.a. |

51

*1897-1913*

| *WORLD* | | | *3.2* | | | *2.0^b 1.3^c* | | |
|---|---|---|---|---|---|---|---|---|
| UK | 4.5 | 1.9 | 3.6 | 1.7 | 1.0 | 1.0^e | 1.2 | -0.2 | -0.1^e |
| Germany | 1.5 | 7.8 | 4.5 | 3.2 | 2.3 | 2.5 | 1.4 | 1.2 | 1.0 |
| USA | 0.8 | 6.5 | n.a. | 4.5 | 2.0 | n.a. | 1.0 | 1.0 | n.a. |
| Italy | 1.6 | 5.0 | n.a. | 2.8 | 2.4 | n.a. | 1.4 | 1.1 | n.a. |
| Sweden | -2.1 | 7.3 | 5.1 | 3.3 | 3.3 | 3.6 | 1.6 | 1.7 | 1.9 |
| Norway | -4.6 | 7.5 | 5.1 | 2.7 | n.a. | n.a. | 1.9 | n.a. | n.a. |
| Denmark | -3.3 | 4.0 | 5.0 | 3.2 | n.a. | n.a. | 0.7 | n.a. | n.a. |

[a]Except for current balances as a percentage of GDP and central bank discount rates which show annual averages. [b]World prices of primary products. [c]World prices of manufactures. [d]1880–1905. [e]1897–1905. n.a. = not available.
*Sources*: World prices – calculated from Lewis (1952). The rest – calculated from the sources given in Table 2.1.

Table 2.3  Differences in economic instability under the classical gold standard (coefficients of variation between different years and countries[a], %)

| | Current balance as % of GDP | Money supply | Central bank discount rates | GDP | Nominal wages Industry | Nominal wages Agriculture | Consumer prices | Real wages Industry | Real wages Agriculture |
|---|---|---|---|---|---|---|---|---|---|
| **1880–1913** | | | | | | | | | |
| *WORLD* | | | | 67.6 | | | 2354.2[b] 2296.6[c] | | |
| UK | 47.1 | 133.0 | 19.2 | 115.3 | 230.7 | 254.7[d] | 4195.2 | 326.5 | 294.5[d] |
| Germany | 39.3 | 86.7 | 20.7 | 57.3 | 93.4 | 89.9 | 331.3 | 152.9 | 258.1 |
| USA | 167.1 | 82.8 | n.a. | 113.1 | 104.5 | n.a. | 1092.4 | 149.8 | n.a. |
| Italy | 285.4 | 95.1 | n.a. | 203.1 | 189.4 | n.a. | 572.9 | 339.5 | n.a. |
| Sweden | 81.7 | 68.1 | 13.9 | 79.0 | 76.5 | 143.3 | 578.9 | 118.7 | 149.0 |
| Norway | 116.0 | 87.6 | 14.9 | 72.8 | n.a. | n.a. | 562.0 | n.a. | n.a. |
| Denmark | 62.2 | 152.2 | 21.3 | 52.4 | n.a. | n.a. | 2820.3 | n.a. | n.a. |
| *Variability between countries* | 269.6 | 40.4 | 11.6 | 30.3 | 38.2 | 73.2 | 80.6 | 37.8 | 73.2 |
| **1880–1896** | | | | | | | | | |
| *WORLD* | | | | 55.4 | | | 232.8[b] 254.0[c] | | |
| UK | 28.2 | 157.3 | 21.2 | 105.6 | 348.4 | 171.8[e] | 202.0 | 141.9 | 180.8 |
| Germany | 30.4 | 130.0 | 17.4 | 60.4 | 106.2 | 175.3 | 537.5 | 147.8 | 360.4 |
| USA | 134.4 | 104.6 | n.a. | 110.5 | 109.5 | n.a. | 284.9 | 81.6 | n.a. |
| Italy | 523.2 | 184.5 | n.a. | 420.1 | 181.9 | n.a. | 3826.8 | 227.0 | n.a. |
| Sweden | 75.4 | 70.1 | 9.4 | 86.4 | 107.8 | 213.7 | 651.5 | 113.0 | 159.2 |

| | | | | | | | | | |
|---|---|---|---|---|---|---|---|---|---|
| Norway | 519.4 | 123.2 | 13.0 | 79.7 | n.a. | n.a. | 363.4 | n.a. | n.a. |
| Denmark | 79.6 | 458.2 | 10.6 | 60.5 | n.a. | n.a. | 254.2 | n.a. | n.a. |
| *Variability between countries* | *3557.1* | *50.4* | *10.5* | *41.7* | *46.2* | *72.8* | *50.0* | *26.9* | *60.8* |
| *1897–1913* | | | | | | | | | |
| *WORLD* | | | | *72.7* | | | *226.6[b] / 265.0[c]* | | |
| UK | 60.4 | 86.3 | 16.8 | 125.9 | 171.7 | 93.7[d] | 157.7 | 856.2 | 2429.4[e] |
| Germany | 44.2 | 48.0 | 16.7 | 53.9 | 79.6 | 41.0 | 123.4 | 157.3 | 178.2 |
| USA | 106.6 | 63.6 | n.a. | 113.8 | 99.0 | n.a. | 197.4 | 272.2 | n.a. |
| Italy | 99.3 | 45.7 | n.a. | 135.8 | 168.7 | n.a. | 225.1 | 466.0 | n.a. |
| Sweden | 85.7 | 51.3 | 11.4 | 69.2 | 49.8 | 100.5 | 150.9 | 118.9 | 126.6 |
| Norway | 37.3 | 59.9 | 11.5 | 62.3 | n.a. | n.a. | 124.0 | n.a. | n.a. |
| Denmark | 42.9 | 53.0 | 14.1 | 44.1 | n.a. | n.a. | 370.2 | n.a. | n.a. |
| *Variability between countries* | *1459.1* | *38.2* | *12.8* | *27.4* | *37.7* | *55.2* | *29.8* | *72.9* | *107.5* |

[a]Refers to country *averages* for each period. [b]World prices of primary products. [c]World prices of manufactures. [d]1880–1905. [e]1897–1905. n.a. = not available.

*Source:* See Table 2.

The next pair of economies, those of the United States and Italy, ran current account deficits for about one-half and one-third of the period respectively. However, instead of alternating – as predicted by the price-specie flow model and 'corroborated' by numerous accounts of the adjustment process under the gold standard – both their deficits and surpluses occurred continuously over long periods. For instance, fourteen of the sixteen US deficits (averaging 1.0 per cent of its GDP) took place between 1882 and 1896; and seven of Italy's ten deficits (averaging 1.9 per cent of the GDP) were incurred between 1884 and 1890. Yet it was only at the end of this prolonged run of deficits that Italy was forced (in 1891) to leave the gold standard. The United States, on the other hand, did not have to experience a similar 'indignity', remaining on the standard throughout its existence.

Finally, what happened to the three Scandinavian countries is even more at odds with the traditional account of how the gold standard worked, as they were almost continuously in deficit on their external trade. Denmark's two surpluses were earned in the first (1880) and the last (1913) year of the period. Norway experienced deficits in every single year between 1890 and the First World War. The deficits were sizeable, around 4.1 per cent of its GDP. In fact, between 1895 and 1909 Norway's current account deficit fell to less than 4.0 per cent of GDP only once (3.5 per cent in 1906). Sweden's seven surpluses were bunched over two short spells: four in the mid 1890s and the rest in the last three years of the period. Hence, like its two neighbours, it was continuously in deficit over many years – with most of the deficits amounting to 3 per cent or more of its GDP.

All this is clearly inconsistent both with the price-specie flow model and with traditional descriptions of how the gold standard 'worked'. Far from being eliminated smoothly and rapidly, current account imbalances under the standard – which were anything but negligible – persisted over many years. Indeed, several countries, all permanent members of 'The Club', were perpetually either in surplus or in deficit throughout the period. Not surprisingly, the behaviour of the other key variables identified in the previous section also contradicts the classical/neoclassical model and countless textbook accounts of the adjustment process under the classical gold standard. The most important among these variables, according to the classical tradition, is the money supply. Following the adjustment process 'mechanisms' described earlier, it should have increased (or grown fastest) continuously in the United Kingdom and Germany and declined (or grown at the lowest rate) in the Scandinavian countries. (The data used here refer to notes and bank deposits in six of the seven countries. The exception is Denmark whose figures exclude bank deposits.) In fact, Table 2.1 shows that there were very few occasions during the period when the quantity of money declined in this particular group of economies. Even more intriguing, this apparently happened more often in the two surplus countries and Italy than in the persistent deficit countries. Contrary to the price-specie flow model, it was Sweden rather than the UK that did not experience a single annual fall in its aggregate quantity of money between 1880 and 1914. As by this time financial innovation had made bank credit by far the most important form of money (Triffin 1964, pp. 51–63), it is not inconceivable that if the relevant data were available they would reveal even fewer, if any, falls in the quantity of money in Denmark than the four shown in Table 2.1. What is more, the growth of money supply was not only more rapid (Table 2.2) but also more stable (Table 2.3) in Sweden and in most of the deficit countries, including Italy, than it was in the UK.

Superficially, this evidence appears to be consistent with one of the basic propositions of the classical model which has survived to this day as 'the monetary approach to the balance of payments' (cf. Frenkel and Johnson 1976). This states that an increase in the quantity of money leads (via higher aggregate demand and inflation) to trade deficit. The problem is that the most rapid annual increases in the quantity of money (nominal or real) occurred in Germany. How did it manage to reconcile this with persistent current account surpluses?

Equally puzzling for anyone taking the classical/neoclassical 'mechanisms' seriously must be the fact that the countries running persistent deficits, and thus losing gold, (a) increased their money supply and (b) having done so year after year, managed (with the exception of Italy) to maintain the value of their currencies fixed to gold and to other currencies!

As indicated in Chapter 1, it was not unusual for members of 'The Club' to take steps to prevent outflows of gold. Alternatively, attempts were made sometimes 'to sterilise' partially the effect of such outflows on their money supply (Bloomfield 1959). However, it is inconceivable that they could have undertaken the evasive action on the scale implied by the data in Tables 2.1–2.3 and remained on the gold standard. The UK's behaviour is no less puzzling. How did it manage to prevent its money supply from growing faster than that in other countries and still maintain the parity of sterling with gold and with other currencies? 'Sterilisation' seems the most obvious answer. But over the years this would have produced a huge increase in UK reserves of gold. In fact, as will be pointed out later, gold reserves held by the Bank of England were very small.

Reasons for the observed inconsistencies will become apparent in the next chapter, which analyses the way in which the adjustment process actually worked under the gold standard. For the moment, it is relevant to notice that the behaviour of the monetary aggregates is supported by that of central bank discount rates for the five countries which had central banks throughout the period. The annual rates, fairly stable in all the countries, were higher in the Scandinavian economies than in the UK and Germany. This is consistent with the relative levels of industrialisation and external balances of the five countries. At the same time, the figures contradict the relevant neoclassical prediction in the sense that average annual discount rates went up more often over the period in the two surplus countries than in the three economies experiencing perpetual current account deficits.

The important conclusion which emerges from this analysis so far is that demand for money appears to have increased rapidly between 1880 and 1913 – especially in the second half of the period – and that the monetary authorities of the countries belonging to 'The Club' were able to meet it even when these countries were running persistent current account deficits. The same appears to be true also of Italy during the two periods (1880–1891 and 1902–14) when it was either formally or informally on the gold standard. Five of its seven contractions in money supply occurred during the 1890s when it was unable to observe the 'rules' of the standard.

Given the paucity of reliable quantitative information for earlier periods, there is, of course, the possibility that the monetary series used here are inadequate to the point of giving a completely misleading impression of financial developments before 1914. This is, however, unlikely for the simple reason that, whatever their limitations, the data present a picture which is consistent with that of the growth and stability of GDP in the seven countries. For it does not require a particularly careful analysis of Tables 2.1–2.3 to notice that while the relative growth of output in these countries is at odds with predictions of the price-specie flow model it is very much in line with the behaviour of the money supply.

As shown earlier, the model predicts that output should either fall or grow more slowly in deficit countries than in surplus ones. More generally, according to the quantity theory of money (one of the cornerstones of the model), if the money supply increases (or grows faster) in country A than in country B – the implication is that A is either prone to greater inflation or that its economy is developing more rapidly and thus requires a greater volume of money for transaction purposes; or, of course, both these things.

What emerges clearly from the first two tables is that, far from persistent trade deficits forcing members of 'The Club' into a state of perpetual economic stagnation, all these countries, unlike Italy, achieved relatively high rates of economic progress. For instance, even during the first half of the period (1880–96), when the world economy was growing appreciably more slowly than after 1896, the US economy developed at a rate well above that of the other countries (Table 2.2) – despite the fact that the country's current balance of payments was almost continuously in deficit.

Denmark and Sweden also achieved impressive economic progress. Denmark was the only country in this particular sample that did not experience a single annual fall in its GDP, followed by Sweden with two falls (Table 2.1). Moreover, in the second half of the period both these countries sustained rates of growth comparable to Germany's and well above the UK's (Table 2.2). Norway's economic development was not as rapid, though it accelerated sharply after 1896, also exceeding appreciably the UK's rate of growth. Yet, as pointed out earlier, this was the period during which the country did not manage to balance its current account in a single year. Apart from their remarkable adaptability to changes in the international economic environment (cf. Jorberg 1973), an important aspect of industrialisation in the Scandinavian countries was its stability (Table 2.3 and Jorberg 1973). As in the case of the United States, there is no indication here that the countries were forced to sacrifice economic welfare as predicted by the classical/neoclassical 'mechanisms'. They quite simply continued to run trade deficits while also being able, apparently without serious difficulties, to keep their currencies fixed to gold and to currencies of other members of 'The Club'.

In fact, it was Italy, the only part-time member of 'The Club', and the UK, the pillar of the whole system, that registered the least impressive growth performances. In the Italian case, this was especially true of the period 1880–96 when it first struggled to stay on the gold standard and then was forced to leave it. Its money supply increased more slowly and showed a greater degree of instability than that of the United States, Sweden and Norway despite the fact that its current account imbalance was much less unfavourable. However, as Tables 2.2 and 2.3 show, Italy's economic performance improved markedly after 1896, enabling it soon afterwards to re-adopt the gold standard and stay on it until 1914.

The growth of the UK economy, on the other hand, slowed

down sharply in the twenty years preceding the First World War, despite a general acceleration in the rate of world economic development. Hence, its economy was the only one in this sample of countries that failed to benefit from a significant improvement in the world economic environment. Yet it was, of course, also the country earning by far the largest current account surpluses. The two facts are easily reconciled within the 'absorption approach to the balance of payments' developed after the Second World War. But they are clearly at odds with the models traditionally used to describe macroeconomic behaviour under the gold standard.

GDP data, like those for the money supply, therefore provide little support for the classical adjustment 'mechanism'. Detailed studies of the cyclical behaviour of gold standard countries confirm this conclusion. They show (cf. Morgenstern 1959) that the cycles were highly synchronised, especially among European countries. In other words, there is no evidence of the 'divergence' between surplus and deficit countries which is one of the key features of the classical adjustment mechanism.

Not surprisingly, the same is also true of nominal wages. To begin with, annual changes in money wages were highly correlated in the three European members of 'The Club'. The coefficients, all statistically significant at the 5 per cent level, were as follows: UK–Germany 0.61, UK–Sweden 0.57 and Germany–Sweden 0.50. Equally important, positive signs in all three cases indicate that there was no divergence over the period between annual wage movements not just in the two surplus economies but also between them and Sweden, one of the most persistent deficit countries. (Although statistically insignificant, comparable correlation coefficients between Italy and the other European countries also have positive signs.) According to the classical adjustment mechanism, the signs should have been negative: with wages increasing in surplus countries (following the expansion in their money supply and output) and falling in deficit countries.

In fact, Table 2.2 shows that nominal wages in both industry and agriculture increased faster in Sweden than in any of the seven countries for which comparable data are available. The Swedes achieved this throughout the entire period of the classical gold standard – despite their persistent current account deficits. Moreover, it is clear from Table 2.3 that variations in the growth of nominal wages were about the same in Sweden as in Germany and appreciably smaller than in the UK.

Lastly, relevant data in Table 2.1 contradict one of the key assumptions behind the classical adjustment model – namely that wages were highly flexible during the period, declining or rising in response to fluctuations in output and demand for labour. Actually, there were very few instances of falls in nominal wage levels – fewer than in GDP levels; and the largest number occurred not, as one might expect, in Italy or Sweden but in the UK. However, even in this case, there were only ten falls in thirty-four years, six of them in the first half of the period. This would suggest a further reduction in downward wage flexibility from the mid 1890s, something that has been confirmed in a number of studies both at the macroeconomic (Phelps Brown and Browne 1968, Gordon 1982, Sachs 1980) and the microeconomic level (Sundstrom 1990). As there is no convincing evidence to contradict this conclusion, it is difficult to see how the adjustment process could have operated among the select group of gold standard countries in the way described by classical and neoclassical economists – unless real wages were much more flexible downwards than nominal ones.

There is certainly a suggestion of this in Table 2.1, as annual reductions in real wages were more common in all five countries for which relevant data are available. Taken together, between 1880 and 1913 the countries experience forty-three falls in real compared to only nineteen in nominal wages. Most of them (thirty out of the forty-three) occurred in the second period when, according to Table 2.2, nominal wages increased in all the countries at a higher rate than before 1896. The implication is that prices rose faster in the second half, which is of course exactly what happened (see below).

Hence, although then (Table 2.4) as now prices and nominal

Table 2.4  Correlations between consumer prices and nominal wages,
1880–1913

|  | Correlation coefficient | t-ratio | Number of observations |
|---|---|---|---|
| **UK** | | | |
| Industrial wages | 0.46[a] | 2.90[a] | 32 |
| Agricultural wages | 0.51[a] | 2.96[a] | 24 |
| **Germany** | | | |
| Industrial wages | 0.47[a] | 3.04[a] | 32 |
| Agricultural wages | 0.32 | 1.95 | 32 |
| **Sweden** | | | |
| Industrial wages | 0.68[a] | 5.20[a] | 32 |
| Agricultural wages | 0.63[a] | 4.62[a] | 32 |
| **USA** | | | |
| Industrial wages | 0.22 | 1.28 | 32 |

[a]Statistically significant at the 5 per cent level.

wages tended to move together, in roughly three out of every ten years price increases outpaced those in money wages in the second sub-period of the classical gold standard. However, generally, the losses were quickly made up in the following year or two so that in the end four out of the five countries experienced increases in real wages during this period also. Sweden again achieved the biggest improvement, though even here the rate of increase was lower than before.

This is not exactly what the classical adjustment model would predict. Nor would it single out the UK as the most likely candidate to experience an overall decline in real wages between 1897 and 1913. Yet the UK was the only country among the five in which that happened. This is hardly surprising, as it was also the only country in this sample in which, according to some estimates, productivity virtually stopped growing, or even declined in the second sub-period (cf. Phelps Brown and Browne 1968, Lewis 1978a, Feinstein 1990). Given the close relationship between rates of growth of output and productivity (Salter, 1966), these findings are consistent with the observed deceleration in the growth of the UK economy.

The problem, of course, is that, except in the case of Germany, all this contradicts the classical adjustment 'mechanism' which would predict performances of the UK and Sweden, in particular, to be exactly the reverse of those which they actually achieved.

Finally, the problem is magnified by the behaviour of prices to an extent that administers nothing less than a *coup de grâce* to the classical model. As explained in the previous section, the model simultaneously eliminates balance of payments surpluses and deficits through changes in relative prices – with the price levels rising in surplus countries and declining in deficit ones. In other words, the restoration of equilibrium in the international economy depends critically on prices in the two groups of economies moving in the *opposite* direction.

In fact, some of the data presented so far point strongly to a completely different conclusion. If annual changes in nominal wages were *positively* correlated in European economies under the classical gold standard, irrespective of their current account positions, and if, in addition, there was a strong *positive* correlation between changes in nominal wages and prices within each country – then it follows that annual movements in their prices also had to be in the *same* direction. Tables 2.5 and 2.6 confirm this in relation to both long- and short-term changes in world and national prices.

The point is so important that it deserves to be illustrated in some detail and (because of data shortcomings) using different price series. As their label indicates, export and import unit values show *unit values* rather than the prices at which goods were traded internationally. Indices of consumer prices are more satisfactory in the sense that they incorporate the actual prices of goods and services. Unfortunately, some of the series available appear to be of particularly poor quality. For instance, the US index of consumer prices was constructed for part of the gold standard period on the assumption that rents (which accounted for 20 per cent of consumer expenditure) were constant. It used wholesale rather than retail prices of food and clothing and assumed that the prices of other items included in the index changed at the same rate as the average of food, clothing and rent (Hoover 1960). It is hardly surprising that in Table 2.1 the US index shows a degree of 'stability' unique among this particular sample of economies. Hence, the three series are useful in providing a partial consistency check on the behaviour of any one indicator of prices in the six gold standard countries and Italy.

Whatever their shortcomings, the three series included in Table 2.5 agree that, far from diverging, prices in both surplus and deficit countries moved together between 1880 and 1913, reflecting broad trends in world prices of primary products and manufactures. They all declined in the first half of the period and rose after 1896. (See also Table 2.2.) Moreover, although, contrary to the belief which still persists, price were highly unstable before 1914 (cf. Table 2.3), the long-term differences between national inflation rates were relatively small, especially in the second sub-period when for most of the time Italy also observed gold standard rules of behaviour.

This is, of course, what one would expect to happen in a system of rigidly fixed exchange rates. It comes, therefore, as no surprise to discover (Table 2.6) that annual variations in both internal and external prices of individual countries were highly and positively correlated with each other and with world prices. The only exceptions are a number of correlations involving US and Italian consumer price indices. The US index, as already pointed out, is highly unreliable. The same is also probably true of the Italian index, though one would expect its prices to be less correlated with those of the other countries. It was after all its propensity to inflate faster than members of the 'The Club' in the first sub-period that forced Italy first to abandon the gold standard and then rejoin it, though only on an informal basis.

McCloskey and Zecher (1976, 1984) have attributed the high correlation between annual changes in national (wholesale) prices during the period to international arbitrage. In conditions of openness and perfect competition, which they assume, the law of one price ensures price uniformity in all markets.

*Table* 2.5   World and national prices, 1880–1913
(annual averages, per cent; coefficients of
variation, %, are shown in brackets)

|  |  | 1880–96 | 1897–1913 |
|---|---|---|---|
| **World** |  |  |  |
| *Primary*: | Food | −1.1 (418.2) | 1.4 (164.3) |
|  | Raw materials | −1.2 (350.0) | 2.5 (320.0) |
|  | All | −1.6 (237.6) | 2.0 (230.0) |
| *Manufactures* |  | −1.2 (216.7) | 1.3 (269.2) |
| **Countries** |  |  |  |
| *UK*: | Consumer goods and services | −1.1 (202.0) | 1.2 (157.7) |
|  | Export unit values | −0.8 (372.4) | 2.0 (255.0) |
|  | Import unit values | −1.6 (218.4) | 1.6 (206.2) |
| *Germany*: | Consumer goods and services | −0.5 (537.5) | 1.4 (123.4) |
|  | Export unit values | −1.8 (372.4) | 0.8 (400.0) |
|  | Import unit values | −2.0 (163.2) | 1.5 (226.7) |
| *USA*: | Consumer goods and services | −0.6 (284.9) | 1.0 (197.4) |
|  | Export unit values | −1.4 (347.4) | 2.2 (250.0) |
|  | Import unit values | −1.2 (403.0) | 1.4 (371.4) |
| *Sweden*: | Consumer goods and services | −0.5 (651.5) | 1.6 (150.9) |
|  | Export unit values | n.a. | 1.9 (207.7) |
|  | Import unit values | n.a. | 0.7 (453.9) |
| *Norway*: | Consumer goods and services | −0.8 (363.4) | 1.9 (124.0) |
|  | Import unit values | −2.2 (142.8) | 1.9 (189.5) |

n.a. = not available.
*Sources*: World prices – Lewis (1952). Consumer prices – Maddison (1982).
Export and import unit values – Maddison (1962).

*Table 2.6* Correlation coefficients between annual changes in national and international prices, 1880–1913 (all the coefficients are statistically significant at the 5 per cent level except those shown in brackets)

| | A | B | *Consumer prices* C | D | E | F | G | H | I |
|---|---|---|---|---|---|---|---|---|---|
| *World prices* | | | | | | | | | |
| A. Primary products | – | | | | | | | | |
| B. Manufacturers | 0.87 | – | | | | | | | |
| *Consumer prices* | | | | | | | | | |
| C. UK | 0.74 | 0.65 | – | | | | | | |
| D. Germany | 0.66 | 0.68 | 0.51 | – | | | | | |
| E. USA | 0.57 | 0.44 | 0.56 | (0.32) | – | | | | |
| F. Italy | (0.31) | (0.24) | (0.29) | 0.44 | (0.28) | – | | | |
| G. Sweden | 0.56 | 0.51 | 0.58 | 0.50 | 0.38 | 0.35 | – | | |
| H. Norway | 0.59 | 0.53 | 0.70 | 0.45 | 0.39 | (0.19) | 0.64 | – | |
| I. Denmark | 0.40 | 0.45 | 0.52 | 0.44 | (0.17) | (0.32) | 0.48 | 0.57 | – |

| | A | B | *Export unit values* C | D | E | F | G | H | I |
|---|---|---|---|---|---|---|---|---|---|
| A. World | – | | | | | | | | |
| B. UK | 0.78 | – | | | | | | | |
| C. Germany | 0.69 | 0.65 | – | | | | | | |
| D. USA | 0.75 | 0.66 | 0.45 | – | | | | | |
| E. Sweden (1894–1913) | 0.74 | 0.68 | 0.75 | 0.61 | – | | | | |

*cont. overleaf*

Table 2.6 continued

Import unit values

| | A | B | C | D | E | F | G | H | I |
|---|---|---|---|---|---|---|---|---|---|
| A. World | – | | | | | | | | |
| B. UK | 0.85 | – | | | | | | | |
| C. Germany | 0.87 | 0.73 | – | | | | | | |
| D. USA | 0.83 | 0.76 | 0.81 | – | | | | | |
| E. Sweden (1894–1913) | 0.95 | 0.84 | 0.91 | 0.80 | – | | | | |
| F. Norway | 0.86 | 0.74 | 0.81 | 0.72 | 0.85 | – | | | |

Each country's export vs. import unit values

| | Correlation coefficient | t-ratio | Number of observations |
|---|---|---|---|
| UK | 0.78 | 6.95 | 34 |
| Germany | 0.55 | 3.63 | 32 |
| USA | 0.62 | 4.44 | 34 |
| Sweden | 0.72 | 4.42 | 20 |

There are several problems with this explanation. Even if one ignores their reliability, overall price indices are constructed in a way that reflects differences in national production, consumption and trading patterns. Moreover, wholesale and consumer prices include both tradeable and non-tradeable goods and services. For these reasons, aggregate price indices are obviously inappropriate for testing the law of one price. In fact, the law cannot be proved even when comparable indices are constructed for specific commodity groups (Kravis and Lipsey 1971 and 1978, Isard 1977). When they happen, adjustments to relative price changes take time, not least because competition in commodity markets is anything but perfect; and the gold standard period saw the emergence and growing importance in many industries of large corporations (Chandler 1977 and 1986, Kemp 1969). Not surprisingly, there are already examples in this period of price fixing between large firms as well as of their control of raw material prices (cf., for instance, Milward and Saul 1977, pp. 50–1).

The explanation offered by Lewis (1978a) – that prices in all these countries were influenced by changes in world agricultural production and trade, notably those of the United States – is therefore much more convincing. Production expanded rapidly in the first half of the period causing agricultural and other prices to fall. Prices went up during the second half when the rate of growth of agricultural production slowed down. Given the positive and statistically highly significant correlation during the period between consumer prices and nominal wages, price increases after 1896 led to higher wages and unit labour costs even in countries such as Germany, the United States and Sweden which experienced an acceleration in the growth of their output and productivity during this period (Phelps Brown and Browne 1968).

Faster growth of output, income and thus demand for both primary products and manufactures, in turn, made it possible for producers to pass on increases in their costs in higher prices. This is consistent with the observation made at the time by Wicksell ([1898] 1936, pp. 157–8). He pointed out that it was changes in foreign supply and demand that influenced 'far more rapidly and far more directly' national price levels, rather than movements of gold.

That being the case, it is difficult to see how national price movements could have diverged significantly or for long; and if they could not do so it was impossible for the classical 'mechanism' to produce the rapid and smooth adjustments still associated with the gold standard.

It is much more likely, therefore, as Ford (1962) has argued, that unforeseen current account deficits were eliminated under the gold standard through changes in employment and income. There are unfortunately no reliable unemployment data that would make it possible to compare the experience of surplus and deficit countries. At the same time, it is clear from output data that reductions in production and income levels (or their rates of growth) could not have been severe or long-lasting in members of 'The Club' experiencing persistent current account deficits. As pointed out earlier, a number of these countries achieved both higher and more stable annual rates of growth than the persistent surplus countries. Hence, although short-term *stabilisation* was almost certainly achieved through policies which affected activity and absorption levels, the *adjustment* process obviously could not have worked in the way traditionally described by classical, neoclassical and Keynesian economists. Clearly, then as now, it took a long time for a country to become capable of eliminating current account deficits without sacrificing output, employment and income.

The important question now is how exactly did deficit members of 'The Club' finance their persistent current account imbalances? As explained in the previous section, the neoclassical extension of the Hume model allowed for the interest rate 'mechanism' and thus the possibility that the deficits could be financed temporarily via short-term capital flows. But is this 'mechanism' any more successful in explaining what actually happened than its price-specie flow equivalent?

## THE EVIDENCE: SHORT-TERM FINANCING

In theory, a country with a large stock of gold and foreign exchange relative to its trade imbalance could run deficits with the rest of the world for years. The larger its reserves, or the smaller its deficits, the longer it could persist with this particular course of action. The mercantilists, of course, knew this; and the need for adequate reserves to protect output and employment was emphasised by Thornton ([1802] 1939) well before the gold standard was adopted by the UK and other countries. The point was restated and elaborated further by Keynes ([1930] 1971) as the interwar experiment with reviving the gold standard was heading towards its inevitable and rather inglorious end.

Monetary authorities can ensure that they have sufficient reserves either by accumulating gold reserves at home and liquid balances in foreign financial centres or by arranging overdraft facilities with other central banks; and these, according to Cassel (1935), were precisely the steps taken by countries on the gold standard, with their central banks maintaining larger reserves than they were legally required to do. Consequently, the balance of payments disequilibria never adjusted automatically and promptly.

This is, no doubt, an accurate explanation of the way that members of 'The Club' financed part of their trade imbalances in the short term – avoiding the abrupt shock to their internal balance that the same model would have produced. The task of both central and commercial banks was made easier in this respect by the fact that during the gold standard period a very high proportion of gold and silver were transferred from public circulation to their reserves. Most of the new gold was also absorbed by banks instead of going into private holdings as had been the case before 1870 (Triffin 1964, p. 19). But could the reserves have been adequate for financing persistent deficits, especially as the latter were far from negligible?

The best way to answer this question is to start by assuming, like the classical economists, that there is no international lending and borrowing. To finance current account deficits amounting to several per cent of its GDP, in such a world a country needs to accumulate in advance large reserves of gold and foreign exchange. In other words, it has to go through a period of earning equivalent current account surpluses and putting these earnings aside in anticipation of the time when its external position becomes reversed. As already mentioned, this is plausible in theory but is there any evidence that it is what actually happened?

One problem with this proposition is that it would have required a degree of long-term national economic planning for which countries on the gold standard had neither the inclination nor the resources. Hence, they clearly must have resorted to something different and more plausible.

Data showing the gold and foreign currency reserves of individual countries are of no greater help in providing a clear answer to the question about the ability of gold standard countries to sustain persistent current account imbalances. For instance, the available evidence shows that international movements of monetary gold were very small between 1880 and 1914. What is more, gold was exported or imported 'predominantly as a result of changes in the banks' need for cash reserves at home and to meet domestic gold-circulation requirement if any, and not as a result of direct changes in the balance of payments' (Bloomfield 1963, p. 48).

If this practice was common, any country dependent solely on the stock of official reserves at its disposal to finance persistent current account deficits would have had to rely for this purpose almost entirely on its holdings of foreign exchange. The problem is that the data collected by Professor Bloomfield show that – with the exception of Sweden, Finland and Belgium – gold accounted for a larger, in some cases considerably larger, proportion of official reserves than did foreign balances (cf. Bloomfield 1963, pp. 17–18).

This can be seen also from Table 2.7. It shows balances of official reserves for five of the seven countries included in this

Table 2.7  Official reserves of gold and foreign exchange, 1880–1913
(millions of US dollars, annual average)

| | Germany | | Sweden | | Norway | | Denmark | | Italy[a] | |
|---|---|---|---|---|---|---|---|---|---|---|
| | I | II | I | II | I | II | I | II | I | II |
| 1880–84 | 57.3 | 3.3 | 3.3 | 7.3 | 6.1 | 2.8 | 13.9 | 2.9 | | |
| 1885–89 | 110.7 | 4.4 | 4.1 | 9.4 | 6.9 | 3.4 | 14.7 | 4.5 | | |
| 1890–94 | 136.7 | 2.7 | 4.8 | 9.3 | 7.4 | 2.4 | 16.1 | 4.0 | | |
| 1895–99 | 145.4 | 4.8 | 7.4 | 15.1 | 8.0 | 3.4 | 18.6 | 2.6 | | |
| 1900–04 | 156.8 | 14.8 | 13.8 | 18.9 | 7.6 | 2.5 | 20.4 | 2.7 | 96.5 | 25.9 |
| 1905–10 | 169.4 | 25.2 | 19.8 | 22.7 | 7.8 | 6.1 | 21.5 | 2.4 | 102.5 | 29.8 |
| 1910–13 | 211.4 | 43.6 | 24.6 | 40.3 | 10.4 | 7.2 | 20.7 | 6.1 | 249.0 | 35.3 |

I = Gold. II = Foreign exchange. [a]Reserves of the three banks allowed to issue notes.
Source: Data supplied by Arthur I. Bloomfield.

book for which relevant data are available. Although there was a general tendency for the proportion of foreign balances to gold to rise towards the end of the period, it was only in Sweden that the balances were consistently a more important component of the official reserves than gold. Hence, had any of these countries financed its persistent current account deficits from official reserves it would have had to export gold; and as a country could not effectively sterilise its outflows of gold *and* remain on the gold standard, it would not have taken long for it to experience deflationary effects of the kind described by Hume.

First of all, however, there would have been a noticeable and continuous change in surplus and deficit countries' reserves, reflecting differences in the state of their current account balances. According to table 2.7, German reserves increased significantly between 1880 and 1913, as one would expect from a country earning persistent current account surpluses. The same applies also to Italy after 1900, a period during which it experienced only three relatively minor current account deficits. What one would not expect to see on the basis of the classical and neoclassical models is that, far from falling, official reserves also increased in the three Scandinavian countries. This is particularly true of Sweden and Denmark whose five-year averages went up consistently throughout the gold standard period. In fact, like the United States, Sweden increased its reserves not only in absolute terms but also relative to imports (Bloomfield 1963, pp. 31–2). Denmark and Norway were less successful in this respect, though they too managed to maintain larger official reserves relative to imports than either the UK or Germany.

UK reserves also present a problem for any model of international exchange which assumes that only goods are traded between countries. For a country earning sizeable current account surpluses year after year, its reserves of gold were surprisingly small. They amounted in 1913 to about 3.4 per cent of the total stock held by the monetary authorities of the thirty-five states for which relevant data exist – well below the reserves of a number of other countries including Russia, Argentina, Italy and Austria-Hungary which were not members of 'The Club' (Lindert 1969, pp. 10–11). The UK was able to get away with such tiny reserves of gold because of confidence in its currency which was widely used in settling international debts. Almost 40 per cent of the world's holdings of official reserves in 1913 were in sterling, well ahead of those denominated in the French franc (24.5 per cent) and the Reichsmark (13.3 per cent) (Lindert 1969, pp. 10–11).

The intriguing thing is that, as explained in the previous section, UK money supply did not increase as rapidly as those of the other six countries analysed here. If its reserves of gold were small and its money supply increased at a low rate, what exactly did it do with its current account surpluses?

One possibility is that the Bank of England had entered into swap arrangements with other central banks, lending to them generously and continuously throughout the gold standard period. The problem is that, for obvious reasons, this kind of arrangement would be unworkable even today, let alone before 1914 when cooperation among central banks left much to be desired.

A notable feature of international monetary arrangements before 1914 was the virtual absence of any systematic cooperation among monetary authorities. Direct contacts among central banks, except in connection with routine banking operations, were very limited. . . . Central bankers showed little or no overt awareness of their mutual responsibility for the smooth functioning of the international gold standard or the need for a collaboration based upon mutual interest (Bloomfield 1963, p. 33).

The Bank of England, the Bank of France and the Reichsbank acted from time to time as international lenders of last resort. Other central banks also extended occasional credits or loans in gold to these three and other central banks in times of crisis (Bloomfield 1959, pp. 56–7, Kindleberger 1978 and 1984, pp. 280–3). The important point is that all of them responded in this way when it was in their national interest to do so rather than because they felt themselves to be under an obligation to assist other economies, or to promote global financial stability. For instance, several times in the 1900s the Bank of France came to the aid of the Bank of England because it did not want the latter to raise its discount rate to even higher levels. This would have made it necessary for the Bank of France to increase its own discount rate, 'a step which for domestic reasons it wanted to avoid' (Bloomfield 1959, p. 57). Central bankers showed a little more awareness of their interdependence after the crisis of 1907 – though this produced no concrete or lasting improvement in their cooperation during the remaining years of the classical gold standard.

In the circumstances, although they cooperated in times of serious crises (Eichengreen 1992), no central bank could have confidently expected other central banks to come to its assistance if it experienced a serious shortage of internationally liquid assets – let alone that they would be prepared to do so regularly over one or more decades. The best that it could hope for was that a major central bank would *occasionally* be willing to help it temporarily. This means that the Scandinavian countries and the United States would never have been able to run current account deficits for years had they depended for the financing of their deficits on the Bank of England, or, indeed, on any other central bank.

This, according to traditional models of balance of payments adjustment and financing under the gold standard, leaves short-term capital flows as the only means of financing persistent current account deficits of the kind described in the previous section. In theory the possibility of short-term borrowing to finance long-term deficits is not as contradictory as it seems. Short-term loans can be rolled over, becoming, in effect, long-term loans. But what about the practice?

Studies of the classical gold standard confirm that interest rates were used by central banks to attract private short-term capital and prevent gold outflows. The frequency with which central banks changed their discount rates depended on their policy objectives and the amount of reserves at their disposal, though the two were not unrelated. For instance, the Bank of France believed that interest rate stability was beneficial to domestic activity. It held large reserves of gold and, if necessary, charged a premium on its gold sales in order to protect its reserves. This means, in effect, that when market developments demanded it, the Bank preferred to suspend free payments in gold partially, rather than alter its interest rate policy. As a result, its discount rate changed only 30 times between 1880 and 1913, compared with 116 and 194 changes made, respectively, by the Reichsbank and the Bank of England over the same period (Ford 1989, p. 236).

Modern writers have expressed serious doubts about the effect of interest rate changes on domestic activity during the period. According to Tinbergen's study of business cycles in the United Kingdom between 1880 and 1914, interest rates exerted 'the chief influence' on investment. However, his estimates indicate that the 'influence' was very modest even in this area: 'The elasticity of investment activity with respect to short-term rates was estimated to be −0.08 and with respect to long term rates to be – 0.50' (Tinbergen 1951, p. 95). Hence, although the transmission mechanism of monetary policy was not well understood before 1914 (cf. Moggridge 1972, chapter 1), the effect of interest rates on activity levels was probably mainly psychological – in the sense that the rates were regarded as an indicator of economic prospects (Bloomfield 1959, Ford 1989). They had, therefore, an effect on the expectation of firms and, consequently, on their actions – both of which took time to change and were also influenced by other considerations.

If this is correct, interest rates were by all accounts much more effective in attracting short-term capital inflows or in preventing outflows. There were, however, important differences. The responsiveness of international short-term capital to changes in interest rates varied a good deal from country to country, depending on confidence in a currency and the range and attractiveness of financial assets available in the country which issued it. The country's level of development relative to the rest of the world, its standing in international financial markets and the diversity and reputation of its financial institutions were therefore of considerable importance.

The UK's pre-eminence in all these respects and its vast short-term claims on foreigners ensured a quick response to changes in the Bank of England's discount rate. Consequently, London could draw funds and gold from Paris and other financial centres, Paris had an advantage over Berlin, and Berlin over other capitals (cf. Lindert 1969, pp. 48–57). It is for this reason that increases in interest rates by countries outside 'The Club', especially those in Latin America, often tended to have exactly the opposite effect from that intended. Instead of preventing outflows of short-term capital, an increase in interest rates would exacerbate them as people became afraid that it would be followed by further increases in interest rates and, eventually, by devaluation.

While this brief description of short-term capital flows during the classical gold standard is undoubtedly correct, it does no more than provide an account of the fact that some countries found it much easier than others to finance their unforeseen current account deficits over very short periods. However, it leaves completely unanswered the question why some countries on the gold standard were able to run current account deficits for most of the period without sacrificing the growth of their economies, incomes and employment.

To be able to rely solely on interest rates to attract short-term funds from abroad would have required the rates to be both higher and rising over time in countries with persistent deficits relative to those prevailing in countries which generally had no problems in reconciling their internal and external balances. Interest rates would need to be higher in the former because the exchange rate risk of lending to them was greater; and they would have to keep rising over time relative to rates elsewhere because the risk was increasing. Persistent and, frequently, very large deficits were bound sooner or later to raise

*Table* 2.8  Central bank discount rates, 1880–1913 (%)

|  | UK | Germany | Sweden | Norway | Denmark |
|---|---|---|---|---|---|
| | | A. *Average annual rates* | | | |
| 1880–84 | 3.6 | 4.0 | 4.4 | 4.4 | 3.8 |
| 1885–89 | 3.6 | 3.2 | 4.0 | 4.0 | 3.2 |
| 1890–94 | 3.3 | 3.5 | 4.5 | 4.7 | 3.7 |
| 1895–99 | 2.8 | 4.0 | 4.6 | 4.5 | 4.2 |
| 1900–04 | 3.6 | 4.2 | 5.0 | 5.4 | 4.8 |
| 1905–09 | 3.7 | 4.7 | 5.3 | 5.0 | 5.3 |
| 1910–13 | 3.9 | 4.9 | 4.9 | 5.0 | 5.2 |
| | | B. *Correlation coefficients*[a] | | | |
| UK | – | | | | |
| Germany | 0.55 | – | | | |
| Sweden | 0.49 | 0.68 | – | | |
| Norway | (0.31) | 0.48 | 0.82 | – | |
| Denmark | 0.46 | 0.76 | 0.92 | 0.77 | – |

[a]All the coefficients are statistically significant at the 5 per cent level or more except the one between UK and Norwegian rates.
*Source*: Calculated from the data collected by Arthur I. Bloomfield.

serious doubts about the ability of deficit countries to sustain their current exchange rates for much longer.

The top half of Table 2.8 shows average levels of annual central bank discount rates for five of the seven countries for which these data are available. The rates are given in a little more detail than in Table 2.2 in order to emphasise the direction of change in their levels between 1880 and 1913. As one would expect, interest rates were lower everywhere in the first half of the period, when prices were falling, than in the second part (especially from the turn of the century until the First World War) when prices rose in all countries (see Table 2.2). Moreover, the rates were higher in the three Scandinavian countries than in Germany and, towards the end of the period, markedly higher in all these countries than in the United Kingdom. At the same time the UK, like the other four countries, experienced an upward trend in its interest rates after 1900. In fact, the jump in the Bank of England's discount rates was very sharp compared to those in the Scandinavian countries. What is more, unlike the UK, Sweden and Norway had lower discount rates in 1910–13 than in 1900–4.

Nevertheless, the impression that one gets is that, broadly, all these rates moved together – a fact which is confirmed by the figures in the lower half of the table. It shows the correlation coefficients of average annual central bank discount rates in the five countries. All the coefficients are highly significant statistically, except the one between the UK and Norwegian rates – indicating that short-term fluctuations in interest rates of 'The Club' countries were highly synchronised. This is, of course, consistent with what one would expect to happen in economies whose monetary systems were integrated and whose business cycles, as mentioned earlier, were also highly synchronised. The importance of the latter is that interest rates in all these countries moved pro-cyclically: they rose in the upturn and fell in the downturn. The reason for this was not that central banks were trying to stabilise the economy. What prompted them to manipulate their discount rates was the fact that they were obliged to do this in order to protect their reserves which tended to fall in the upturn and rise in the downturn (Bloomfield 1959, pp. 37–9). This, plus international arbitrage, made it very difficult for a country on the gold standard to get out of step, except in the very short term.

The significance of this evidence is that it makes it impossible for 'the interest rate mechanism' to secure adequate external finance to cover persistent current account deficits. If money markets in countries on the gold standard were highly integrated and subject to international arbitrage, it is difficult to see how any one of them could have used interest rate differentials to attract short-term capital except in the very short run. Given the existence of a distinctive hierarchy of markets, described earlier, this would have been particularly true of deficit countries like Sweden, Norway and Denmark which were some way down in the international financial 'pecking' order. Short-term capital flows – like official gold and foreign currency reserves, and borrowing from other central banks – could not, therefore, have financed persistent current account deficits.

*Table* 2.9    Sweden: current account balances, short-term capital flows and
official reserves, 1880–1913
(five-year totals in million kroner)

|  | *(1)*<br>*Current account*<br>*balances* | *(2)*<br>*Net short-term*<br>*capital flows*[a] | *(3)*<br>*Difference:*<br>*(1)−(2)* | *(4)*<br>*Official reserves*<br>*of gold and*<br>*foreign exchange* |
|---|---|---|---|---|
| 1880–84 | −257 | 8 | −249 | 198 |
| 1885–89 | −315 | −15 | −330 | 252 |
| 1890–94 | −144 | −21 | −165 | 263 |
| 1895–99 | −114 | − 8 | −122 | 420 |
| 1900–04 | −399 | 21 | −378 | 610 |
| 1905–09 | −417 | 51 | −366 | 793 |
| 1910–13 | 78 | −155 | − 77 | 969 |

[a]Minus sign = net outflows.
*Sources*: Mitchell (1975) and Bloomfield (1968).

This can be seen from Table 2.9 which gives quinquennial
totals of current account balances, net short-term capital flows
and official reserves for the one country, Sweden, for which all
these series of data are available. Clearly, short-term capital
inflows would have been completely inadequate to finance the
country's persistent current account deficits. The same applies
also to official reserves in the 1880s. Equally important, the
figures in column 3 cannot be reconciled with continuous and
often substantial increases in the country's official reserves of
gold and foreign exchange. Other things being equal, Sweden
should have run out of reserves at the beginning of the period,
with no option but either to abandon the gold standard or
follow a policy of perpetual deflation and economic stagnation.

The Swedes would probably have had to make this choice
very soon after adopting the gold standard for the simple
reason that then as now short-term capital flows could be
highly destabilising. In the case of gold standard countries the
flows were sufficiently large to make it impossible for the
authorities to keep their exchange rates fixed. But the flows
could also be large in the case of gold standard countries if
there were any doubts about their ability to stay on the stan-

dard (Bloomfield 19763, pp. 83–9). The United States experienced this in the 1890s, forcing it to impose temporary exchange controls in 1895; and Russia had, for the same reason, to resort briefly to such controls in 1907 following its war with Japan (Bloomfield 1959, pp. 58–9).

## CONCLUSIONS

The most important conclusion to emerge from the evidence presented in this chapter is that had the classical gold standard really depended for its existence entirely on the price-specie flow and interest rate 'mechanisms', as the traditional accounts of its operation lead one to believe, it would have never got off the ground; or, alternatively, if it had been adopted *and* lasted, it would have been a period of perpetual stagnation in most members of 'The Club'. Instead, the system survived for over three decades, a period during which all these countries achieved a radical transformation of their economies. What is more, few members of 'The Club' were more successful in this than those that apparently 'broke' the rules of 'responsible behaviour' normally associated with the period.

The next chapter explains why the select few were able 'to get away' with such behaviour. In doing so, it provides what is undoubtedly the most important lesson for the survival of all fixed exchange rate regimes and, even more relevant, for the long-term viability of an international monetary system.

# 3 The Secret of the Gold Standard's Durability and Success

The analysis in the previous chapter was deliberately confined to the current account and short-term capital flows in accordance with traditional, static models of the adjustment and financing processes under fixed exchange rate systems in general and the classical gold standard in particular. It showed conclusively that the standard never operated in the way described by the classical/neoclassical models. The synchronisation of short-term movements in national prices and interest rates was such that the 'mechanisms' analysed in the last chapter could not have produced either lasting adjustments or long-term financing of the kind attributed to them by the conventional wisdom. It is necessary, therefore, to look for other explanations why this, the most exacting of all quasi international monetary unions, managed to survive for so long.

Few, if any, contemporaries would have had serious doubts about the 'real' reason for this: adherence to the standard was responsible for the dynamism and success of the economies which observed rigidly 'the rules' throughout its existence. Consequently, there was no reason for them even to contemplate alternative monetary arrangements. However, it turns out on closer examination that it was not the standard's contribution to the long-term progress of their economies that made powerful economic interests in countries belonging to 'The Club' persevere with the system but rather the fact that, in their case at least, 'membership' did not interfere with the major economic changes to which they were strongly committed. With the possible exception of the United Kingdom after the mid 1890s, they did not have to sacrifice industrial development and economic welfare in order to participate in the international monetary union. This was, of course, particularly relevant for countries running persistent current account deficits.

How exactly did they manage to avoid the permanent stagnation to which the price-specie flow mechanism might otherwise have condemned them?

## THE THREE PILLARS OF THE CLASSICAL GOLD STANDARD

To answer this question, it is necessary to analyse three important developments which took place during the period. These developments enabled a select group of countries to transform their economies and improve markedly their economic welfare. In doing so, they prevented the classical gold standard from disintegrating as dramatically as did the short-lived attempt to revive it between the two world wars. The three developments were: the greatest volume (in relation to national incomes at the time) of international investment on record; an equally unparalleled level of international migration; and a differentiation of national trade policies in accordance with differences in levels of industrialisation and, therefore, in the needs of individual economies.

Each of these factors was associated with profound dynamic changes in a number of countries and, as a result of this, in the international economic system as a whole. The international movement of labour and national commercial policies influenced the scale and speed of the desired long-term adjustments. International investment, on the other hand, made such adjustments possible by transferring productive resources and knowledge from surplus to deficit countries. Where the combination of these factors was inadequate to make sustained industrialisation possible, the countries involved either could not adopt the gold standard or, if they did so, were unable to stay on it for very long.

This explains 'The Club's' exclusiveness. In modern terminology, it consisted of economies capable of pursuing policies that would in the long term enable them to reconcile their internal and external balances – with the latter referring to the *basic* (current plus long-term capital accounts) rather than just current balances of payments.

That, of course, is not an explanation that would have made much sense to those operating the classical gold standard. Deliberate reconciliation of internal and external balances became a major objective of economic policy only several decades and two world wars later. At the same time, there was nothing 'spontaneous' about the determined effort which these countries made to industrialise. Governments, backed up by powerful commercial interests, played a major role in the process (Supple 1973, Sen 1984, Milward and Saul 1977, Mathias and Pollard 1989) mainly for political reasons: (a) to protect the sovereignty of their countries and thus their own pre-eminence enshrined in the existing institutional framework; and (b) to regain, or achieve, some influence in shaping a world which was rapidly changing beyond all recognition.

The United Kingdom's rise to global superiority convinced many countries that they needed considerable military power to achieve these two objectives; and this was impossible in the second half of the nineteenth century without a strong industrial base. This probably explains better than anything else the rush to industrialise which occurred during the period. That being the case, it is inconceivable that governments determined to see their countries achieve sustained economic progress for such a reason would willingly have accepted the 'discipline' of an international monetary union, even of the quasi variety, unless this was in their national interest.

As it turned out, a unique complementarity of factor endowments and needs enabled a number of them ('The Club') to undertake successful industrialisation within an internationally integrated monetary and economic framework. Adopting the standard was equivalent to establishing a permanent line of communications with the capital and money markets of other countries – particularly those of the UK, France and Germany. This link assured the markets that borrowers from a country whose currency was tied to gold would observe certain rules of behaviour demanded by international creditors; and, *ceteris paribus*, provided that the markets responded by lending generously, the country was indeed able to realise this expectation. Otherwise, as the experience of many nations shows, the link could not be maintained.


## THE DYNAMICS OF THE ADJUSTMENT PROCESS

The importance of international links in making it possible for members of 'The Club' to achieve their internal economic objectives and, at the same time, balance their external accounts can be illustrated with the help of a simple model. It is based on the analytical framework developed originally by Harrod (1948) and Domar (1957) in their analysis of the conditions required to achieve and maintain full employment in an advanced, closed capitalist economy. To establish this, Harrod made a distinction between three rates of economic growth, only two of which are required for the analysis in this chapter.

The first of these rates, potential (or 'natural', as he called it), is defined as

$$y_p = l + y/l \tag{1}$$

where $y_p$ = the rate of growth of potential output, $l$ = the rate of growth of the labour force and $y/l$ = technical progress reflected in the rate of growth of labour productivity.

In an economy operating at full employment, $y_p$ is obviously the highest attainable rate of growth. In other words, it cannot be exceeded by actual growth ($y_a$). However, in an economy with a good deal of unemployment, $y_a > y_p$ is possible until it reaches full employment. In this case, $y_p$ is clearly the *minimum* short-term rate of growth that must be achieved to prevent increasing unemployment.

The obvious question now is: what conditions have to be satisfied to ensure that $y_a \geq y_p$? In practice, $y_a$ is invariably the outcome of a whole host of complex economic, social and political factors, with their relative importance varying from country to country. There are, however, two rather 'simple' macroeconomic conditions that have to be fulfilled in every case: the volume of investment has to be sufficiently high for $y_a$ to equal $y_p$; and that is possible only if the volume of savings is equal to the required volume of investment. The exact size of new savings and investment needed to achieve this will depend partly on the required rate of growth and partly on the amount of capital needed to produce additional output.

The capital–output ratio will be determined by the level of development achieved by an economy and by its structure. As these cannot be changed easily, whether or not the required rate of economic growth is reached in the short run will depend entirely on the volume of savings (and investment) generated by an economy. (It is assumed, of course, that savings and investment are always equal *ex post*.) Consequently, the actual rate of growth ($y_a$) can be defined as

$$y_p = s/c \tag{2}$$

where $s =$ the proportion of national income saved and $c =$ the incremental capital–output ratio.

Suppose, for instance, that an economy is operating at full employment with $y_a = y_p$. Then, having managed this for many years, it begins to copy rapidly the technical and organisational advances made by countries which have achieved a significantly higher level of industrialisation. There will be two effects. First, the rate of growth of labour productivity will accelerate. Second, health standards will improve, reducing the country's mortality rate and thus increasing the rate of growth of its population and the labour force. Consequently, the country will have a new potential rate of growth of

$$(y_p)_n = (l)_n + (y/l)_n \tag{3}$$

where $(y_p)_n > y_p$, $(l)_n > l$ and $(y/l)_n > y/l$, with subscript 'n' referring in each case to the new period.

This means that in order to avoid an increase in unemployment, the country must achieve a higher actual rate of growth. That is, the change requires $(y_a)_n > y_a$. Otherwise, unemployment will rise – creating eventually serious social problems and political instability which will jeopardise the country's effort to industrialise.

The important condition implicit in these changes is that the level of investment has to increase, which means that the savings ratio has to go up even if the capital-output ratio remains constant:

$$(y_a)_n = (s)_n/c \tag{4}$$

where $(s)_n > s$. If $c$ also becomes higher – which is not inconceivable if the country has to invest heavily in the infrastructure – then $(s)_n$ will need to be even greater.

Raising the savings rate is far from easy to achieve in the short run. Consumers may wish to copy the consumption patterns of the more advanced countries, which will reduce the level of personal savings. Most domestic firms are likely to be run inefficiently, generating too low profits to finance major investment projects internally. The financial system will be insufficiently advanced to inspire the sort of confidence that will enable it to attract savings at interest rates which are not so high as to discourage investment. This leaves the government sector. Government, after all, can increase the savings ratio through taxes. The problem is that at low levels of development the taxable capacity of an economy is small; and so also is the government's competence to maximise its revenue from the limited resources at its disposal. For all these reasons, the *domestic* level of savings may fall short of that needed for $y_a$ to equal, let alone exceed, $y_p$.

Take, for instance, the case of an economy whose labour force is growing at 1 per cent and productivity at 1.5 per cent. (These two and the other rates given in this section refer to *annual* growth.) That gives $y_p$ = 2.5 per cent. Assuming that $c$ = 3, the economy will be able to keep its level of unemployment unchanged if $s$ = 7.5 per cent. Assuming further that this is the case, $y_a$ will also be 2.5 per cent, so that $y_a$ = $y_p$.

However, suppose that the country now makes a major, sustained effort to industrialise by absorbing the best practice techniques used in other countries. As a result, the growth of its labour supply accelerates from 1 to 1.5 per cent and the growth of productivity from 1.5 to 3.5 per cent – doubling $y_p$ from 2.5 to 5 per cent. Assuming that $c$ remains 3, this requires $s$ to double, from 7.5 to 15 per cent. But if heavy expenditure on the infrastructure, which is normally highly capital intensive, raises $c$ to (say) 4, $s$ will have to be increased to 20 per cent of the national income. This is a tremendous effort, probably well beyond the country's capacity in the short run, given its efficiency and income levels.

Let us assume, therefore, that it manages to do no better than $s$ = 14 per cent. If $c$ = 3 this gives $y_a$ = 4.7 per cent. The result is a rise in unemployment as investment cannot be increased to the level needed to achieve $(y_a)_n$ = 5 per cent. The only way to avoid higher unemployment is to reduce $(y/l)_n$ from 3.5 to 3.2 per cent if $c$ = 3 and to 2 per cent if $(c)_n$ = 4. In other words, the country can avoid higher unemployment only by settling for lower increases in productivity and incomes than those of which it is capable. Given that domestic savings are constrained to a maximum of 14 per cent of national income, attempts to raise the investment ratio above this level will, of course, only cause an acceleration in the rate of inflation – without closing the gap between the actual and potential rates of growth.

In fact, once the assumption of a closed economy, implicit in the preceding analysis, is dropped – the situation is likely to be even more serious. A country is most unlikely to be able to adopt best practice techniques from abroad without acquiring capital equipment and technical and managerial expertise from those economies whose development model it is trying to replicate. This will cause its imports to grow rapidly. At the same time, it may not find it possible to expand exports in the short run to pay for higher imports: the country's productive capacity is likely to be too limited to achieve this. Moreover, the price and income elasticities of foreign demand for its products may not be sufficiently high to enable it to balance its current balance of payments. Consequently, it is unlikely to be long before domestic savings $(S_d)$ are exceeded by domestic investment $(I_d)$ and exports $(X)$ by imports $(M)$, giving a current account deficit, since within the national income framework

$$I_d > S = M > X \tag{5}$$

For reasons analysed in the previous chapter, this cannot be sustained for long. The reserves will rapidly run out; and short-term loans cannot be expected to finance long-term development. The country's $y_a$ will therefore be restricted to a rate significantly lower than $(y_p)_n$ unless it can attract long-term investment $(LTC)$ from abroad. The importance of this is that $LTC$ adds foreign savings $(S_f)$ and thus foreign investment $(I_f)$ to those generated from domestic savings, raising the overall level of domestic investment and, at the same time, making it possible through greater availability of foreign exchange to finance the imports without which domestic development could not be achieved (see McKinnon 1964, Rosenstein-Rodan 1961). In other words, the disequilibrium can be avoided if

$$I_r - S_d = S_f \tag{6}$$

where $I_r$ = the level of investment that has to be sustained for $(y_a)_n = (y_p)_n$. In terms of the balance of payments identity, $S_f = LTC$ so that (6) becomes

$$I_r - S_d = M - X = LTC \tag{7}$$

In an open economy, the actual rate of growth in (3) can be re-written as

$$(y_a)_n = (s_{d+f})_n /c \tag{8}$$

Thus, going back to the example given earlier, even if $s_d =$ 14 per cent and $(c)_n = 4$, and provided that, on average, $s_f = 6$ per cent of the country's national income over a number of years, the country will be able to raise its investment level (assumed to equal $s_d + s_f$) to the 20 per cent required to sustain $(y_p)_n = 5$ per cent. At the same time, it will have no external problems as the basic balance of payments will be in balance. (Incidentally, the example of $s_f = 6$ per cent may seem too high as it implies that foreigners are financing no less than 30 per cent of the country's fixed capital formation. However, as will be shown in the next section, the figure is not without historical precedent.)

The emigration of labour can also prevent rising unemployment, acting as an alternative to foreign investment. This is obviously particularly important in the case of countries that find it difficult to raise the required amount of capital on international financial markets.

Provided that a sufficient number of people emigrate each year over a longer period, a country's $(l)_n$ and therefore $(y_p)_n$ will be reduced to more manageable levels – assuming that $(y/l)_n$ does not accelerate. The reason for this is that emigration will reduce $I_r$ (and also, of course, imports). As a result of lower rates of growth of population and hence of the labour force, a smaller proportion of national income will have to be invested not just to raise industrial capacity but also in housing and social capital (roads, railways, airports, sewage and water systems, telephone and telegraph, schools, hospitals etc.). Moreover, by diminishing the need for investment in infrastructure, emigration may also reduce $c$, making it even easier to achieve or, if necessary, exceed $(y_p)_n$.

Take, for instance, the earlier example in which $s_d = 14$ per cent, $(c)_n = 4$ and $(y/l)_n = 3.5$ per cent. Now, however, thanks to large-scale emigration, instead of accelerating to 1.5 per cent, $(l)_n$ falls to 0.5 per cent. This brings $(y_p)_n$ down from 5 to 4 per cent, which is attainable provided that $(s)_n = 16$ per cent. With $s_d = 14$ per cent, the required savings (and thus investment) ratio can now be reached with the much more modest foreign investment of $s_f = 2$ per cent, instead of the $s_f = 6$ per cent needed before. In fact, if lower investment in the infrastructure were to reduce $(c)_n$ from 4 to 3.5, a domestic savings ratio of 14 per cent would be sufficient to enable the country to achieve $(y_p)_n$ without running current account deficits. In this case $S + M = I + X$, eliminating the need for net inflows of $LTC$.

What this example shows is that, at least in theory, international migration and investment can be perfect substitutes. The important implication is that the greater the barriers to international labour mobility within a monetary union, the greater will international investment need to be if individual countries, and the union as a whole, are to realise their productive potential and thus maximise economic welfare. Alternatively, the greater the volume of international investment the lower will be the need for international migration within the union.

Finally, the greater the barriers to global factor mobility the greater will be the pressure on deficit countries to insulate their economies through trade restrictions and exchange controls in order to realise $(y_p)_n$. Protection has, of course, many different aspects. Its financial importance is that by reducing imports of goods it economises on foreign exchange provided by net inflows of $LTC$. At the same time, it boosts $s_d$ (a) through forced savings (generated by higher prices) which raise the level of corporate profits, and (b) by ensuring, where protection includes controls on capital exports, that savings accumulated within an economy are used for domestic investment only. *Ceteris paribus*, protection thus makes it possible to increase the level of actual investment $(I_a)$ towards that of $I_r$. In other words, it raises a country's capacity to reconcile its internal and external balances. Hence, the greater the obstacles to international movements of labour and investment the more important is the role of protection in the international adjustment process likely to be.

There is, however, one aspect of protection which is normally overlooked. For the dynamic adjustment process to produce the results described so far in this section, it is essential that levels of protection should be progressively reduced as levels of efficiency and income rise. At the highest level, the most advanced economies – which normally tend to earn persistent current account surpluses even at full employment – should have no restrictions on either trade or capital flows. Otherwise, the international adjustment process will break down, with widespread losses of welfare.

Basically, this can happen in either of the following two ways. First, if surplus countries restrict exports of long-term capital and immigration of foreign labour, the first two routes by which deficit countries can achieve the long-term adjustment described above will be closed to them. As pointed out earlier, their $s$ will be insufficient to realise and sustain $I_r$ so that $y_a < (y_p)_n$. To make things worse, $c$ may rise appreciably: partly because of the need for greater investment in the infrastructure and partly because of the inferior nature and inefficient use of new investment, as they will be unable to pay for the superior capital equipment and technical know-how available in the more advanced (surplus) countries.

Second, the position of deficit countries may become even worse if surplus countries allow freedom of capital movement but continue to control immigration tightly and restrict imports of goods. This particular combination of policies, in fact, reduces significantly the capacity of deficit countries to raise $LTC$ abroad. The reason for this is that restrictions on their exports make it virtually impossible for them to acquire the foreign exchange needed to service and repay loans of the size required to raise $y_a$ at least to the level of $(y_p)_n$. The gap between $y_a$ and $(y_p)_n$ will become even wider if deficit countries underestimate the seriousness of the problem and borrow on the international financial markets a volume of capital in excess of the prudential limit imposed by surplus countries' policies. In such a case, they would have to keep actual growth well below that of $(y_p)_n$ in order to reduce even essential imports. This is the only way in which they could generate sufficient current account surpluses to service and repay their external debts.

In conclusion, the analysis in this section has important policy implications for an international monetary union such as that formed by those who adopted the classical gold standard. Assuming that countries at different levels of development join it, the extent to which they can observe the rules and, at the same time, achieve their domestic objectives will, *ceteris paribus*, depend on the combination of policy approaches just described. The smaller the volume of international investment from surplus to deficit countries the larger will have to be labour migration in the opposite direction and the higher will be protection levels. Alternatively, if migration is negligible the scale of protection will depend on the size of international investment in the deficit countries. The latter will have to be especially large if members of the union are required to pursue a policy of free trade irrespective of differences in their efficiency and income levels. Otherwise, deficit countries will have no alternative but to eliminate current account deficits by sacrificing economic welfare – exactly as specified in the Hume model. As emphasised in the previous two chapters, few countries were either able or willing to do this even under the classical gold standard.

The important question, therefore, is: how did the three factors described in this chapter allow the less industrialised members of 'The Club' who ran persistent current account deficits to avoid the full rigours of the price-specie flow 'mechanism'?

## INTERNATIONAL INVESTMENT

Relative to the size of the capital exporting countries, the volume of international investment between 1880 and 1914 has never been approached let alone equalled. Bairoch's (1976, p. 99) estimates put it around 4 per cent of the countries' GNP in 1870, rising to almost 5 per cent of their combined GNP in 1913. The highest comparable figure since then was reached in 1960 when the ratio exceeded slightly 1 per cent (Panić 1988, p. 172).

As one would expect, most of this investment came from the three countries (UK, France and Germany) which were running persistent current account surpluses by generating savings in excess of domestic investment and exports. This was especially true of the UK (cf. Cairncross, 1953). In the 1900s it even managed (Table 3.1) to invest a higher proportion of its savings abroad than at home – something that no other country has ever done. Given that the UK economy at this time was second in size only to that of the United States, it is hardly surprising to discover that it accounted for the bulk of international investment before 1914: 42 per cent of the total, well in excess of the French (20 per cent) and German (13 per cent) investments put together (Woytinsky and Woytinsky 1955, p. 191).

Consequently, although the contribution of France and Germany, one-third of the total, was far from negligible, it was the UK that dominated the international financial system before 1914. In fact, given the size and range of its operations, the City of London was virtually *the* international capital market. This meant that apart from generating larger excess savings and current account surpluses than any other country, the UK also provided a framework of financial institutions willing and able to intermediate globally between savers and investors. The expertise and reputation of these institutions were such that it was not unusual for savers from other countries to lend to borrowers in their own country through UK banks in London.

International movements of long-term capital were influenced then, as now, by long-term considerations, rather than by short-term changes such as those in interest rates. Although annual volumes of international investment tended to vary according to the state of the business cycle in both capital exporting and capital importing countries (Kindleberger 1985, Triffin 1964, Bloomfield 1968), the more successful a country was in sustaining a high rate of growth relative to the rest of the world the more likely it was to attract international investment. There were two reasons for this: greater domestic demand for foreign capital and a greater readiness on the part of foreign investors 'to invest in these countries in view of the more favourable economic prospects and anticipated rates of

Table 3.1 Gross savings and domestic and foreign investment[a] as a percentage of gross national product (three-year averages centred on the years shown)

| | Domestic savings | | | | Domestic fixed investment | | | | Foreign investment[b] | | | |
|---|---|---|---|---|---|---|---|---|---|---|---|---|
| | 1880 | 1890 | 1900 | 1910 | 1880 | 1890 | 1900 | 1910 | 1880 | 1890 | 1900 | 1910 |
| UK | 11.4 | 12.9 | 12.2 | 14.1 | 8.2 | 7.2 | 10.4 | 6.7 | -3.2 | -5.7 | -1.8 | -7.4 |
| France | 19.4 | 21.3 | 25.2 | 24.6 | 19.8 | 19.3 | 21.3 | 21.0 | 0.4 | -2.0 | -3.9 | -3.6 |
| Germany | 10.1/ | 14.2/ | 16.3/ | 15.4/ | 8.1 | 12.2 | 15.0 | 14.0 | -1.9 | -2.0 | -1.3 | -1.3 |
| Italy | 10.9 | 8.7 | 14.2 | 15.0 | 9.8 | 9.1 | 12.0 | 15.1 | -0.7 | 0.4 | -2.2 | 0.1 |
| USA | 20.1 | 23.2 | 23.2 | 20.9 | 20.0 | 23.7 | 21.8 | 20.9 | -0.1 | 0.1 | -1.4 | 0.0 |
| Sweden | 9.2 | 9.2 | 11.6 | 13.8 | 11.0 | 10.3 | 13.8 | 13.1 | 3.7 | 2.5 | 2.7 | -0.4 |
| Canada | n.a. | 8.7 | 9.2 | 12.8 | n.a. | 15.7 | 13.2 | 25.3 | n.a. | 7.0 | 4.0 | 12.0 |
| Australia | 13.5 | 10.1 | 11.9 | 16.0 | 19.0 | 17.2 | 15.3 | 15.2 | 0.1 | 0.1 | 0.0 | 0.0 |

[a]Outflows = −. Inflows = +. Net savings = /. [b]The figures are not equal to the difference between domestic savings and fixed investment in several cases because of differences in the periods covered by the data.
Source: Green and Urquhart (1976).

return – unless perhaps opportunities happened to be more favourable in the investing countries themselves' (Bloomfield 1968, p. 15). This, in turn, enabled such countries to sustain a rapid rate of industrialisation.

It is not surprising, therefore, that among deficit economies a country like Sweden – rich in natural resources and possessing a highly educated and dynamic labour force – for years attracted foreign investment and grew rapidly (Sandberg 1979); or that, among surplus economies, German investors had less incentive than their British and French counterparts to look for profitable opportunities outside their own country. The experience of nations with unsuccessful economies and unattractive economic prospects was, of course, exactly the reverse. Virtuous *and* vicious circles were at least as common then as they are today.

What is unusual about these movements in the period 1880–1914 is the extent of complementarity between capital exporting and capital importing countries. The industrialisation of Western Europe and growth of its population increased demand for food and raw materials. The problem was that none of the countries was self-sufficient in these products, especially the UK. Their further economic progress and improvements in the standard of living depended, therefore, on adequate supplies of primary products from the rest of the world. As it happened, agricultural land and raw materials were abundant in the sparsely populated countries of the Americas and Oceania, as well as in parts of Northern and Eastern Europe. The problem was that most of these resources were inaccessible and undeveloped. To overcome this problem, countries rich in natural resources needed foreign investment and know-how. Those in America and Oceania were also short of labour. As a result, international investment during the gold standard period was largely complementary. It promoted international specialisation between industrial countries in Western Europe and primary producing economies in other parts of Europe and the world.

In other words, international flows oi long-term capital were essential for the development of both the industrial core and the primary producing countries anxious to industrialise. Each group provided the most important market for the other group's exports, as these consisted of products which were of critical importance for the importers' own development.

It is this complementarity and interdependence which also explain the relative concentration of international investment. It not only originated in a small number of countries but also went predominantly to a small group. Apart from their ability to produce the kind of foodstuffs and raw materials demanded by the lending economies, the most successful borrowing countries shared a number of other characteristics: a sufficiently large market to absorb manufactured imports, adequate transport and communication facilities, trained manpower, a developed administrative apparatus and, finally, the capacity to organise modern production and distribution processes and networks.

This explains why a very high proportion of foreign investment during the gold standard period went to the wealthiest and/or economically most successful countries: the United States, Canada, Australia and, in Europe, the Scandinavian countries and, in the second half of the period, Russia and Austria-Hungary (cf. Bairoch 1976, Bloomfield 1968, Woodruff 1982, Fishlow 1985). Between them, North America and Europe absorbed over half the long-term capital flows before 1914. In addition to promising attractive returns, the risks associated with investments on these two continents and Oceania were lower than in other parts of the world. Most international investment outside the three continents just mentioned went – mainly in the second half of the period – to countries, such as those in Latin America, which attracted a high proportion of European settlers and appeared to have the potential for successful long-term development.

Some of the investments before 1914 were in the form of government loans used for military purposes. This was especially true of French and German lending to Russia and countries in central and southern Europe. A far greater proportion, however, went into the construction of railways. For instance, almost 60 per cent of US borrowing before the First World War was for this purpose (cf. Segal and Simon 1961, Simon 1967, Lewis 1938, p. 546). Public investment also attracted a substantial share of foreign capital, enabling borrowing countries to develop their infrastructure. It went into public utilities, the construction of roads, bridges and public buildings, and the development of communication facilities such as telegraph and telephone networks. The investments were obviously essential for the development of these economies. In addition, they played an important role in linking them more closely with the highly industrialised creditor countries in Western Europe.

These investments also shared two important characteristics. First, international loans tended to be raised mainly in the form of bonds with very long maturities, often extending over many decades. Even bonds with maturities of up to ninety-nine years were 'not uncommon' (World Bank 1985, p. 13). This gave borrowing countries the chance to undertake capital projects of the kind just described: with long gestation periods and, therefore, incapable of producing quickly a high rate of return on the capital invested.

Second, although investment in railways and other forms of the infrastructure was carried out in the receiving countries mainly by private companies, this was made possible by government assistance in the form of guarantees, land loans and cash grants. According to Bloomfield (1968, p. 4): 'the bulk of the international long-term borrowing in the period before 1914 depended directly or indirectly on government action in the capital importing countries'. This was certainly true of the Unites States, the Scandinavian countries and Italy (cf. Lewis 1938, Letwin 1989 Wilkins 1989, Jorberg 1973, Jonung 1984, Milward and Saul 1977).

The investment described so far was 'portfolio': the acquisition by residents of capital exporting countries of bonds and shares issued by governments and private enterprises in borrowing countries. However, direct investment (used by firms of one country either to establish or to acquire one or more enterprises in another country, managed and controlled by the investing firm) also became important during the period analysed here. According to Dunning (1988, p. 72), by 1914 direct investment 'represented about 35 per cent of the estimated total long-term debt at that time'.

Most of the direct investment went into primary production (55 per cent of the total) and manufacturing (15 per cent of the total). Over 80 per cent of the latter was located in Europe (predominantly Western Europe) and North America (US and Canada) (Dunning 1988, pp. 73 and 77) – in other words, the most advanced economies. Several factors were responsible for the spread of direct investment in manufacturing at this time. A widespread increase in tariffs was one of them. Even more important, improvements in transport and communications and the appearance of industries dependent on economies of large-scale production made it both possible and profitable for firms to operate in more than one country. Combined, these changes facilitated the formation of transnational enterprises – though the risk of failure remained high throughout the period (see Wilkins 1989).

Misallocation and misuse of international investment, defaults and financial crises were, of course, not uncommon before 1914 (cf. Kindleberger 1978, Fishlow 1985). But they affected lending to individual countries rather than the overall volume of international investment.

There were probably three reasons for this. First, a defaulter would find it impossible for quite some time afterwards to raise loans on the international capital markets. Few countries were, therefore, prepared to take such a decision lightly. Second, it was not unusual for creditor nations to take direct steps to enforce debt contracts. In most cases they appear to have been equivalent to a vigorous enforcement (often by foreign commissioners) of measures reminiscent of IMF 'conditionality', though force was also used occasionally (Foreman-Peck 1983, chapter 5; Milward and Saul 1977, p. 497). The third and, no doubt, most important reason for such a large volume of international investment was its importance to both lending and borrowing countries.

Lending countries, as already mentioned, secured through their exports of capital a steady supply of raw materials and foodstuffs as well as the creation of new, rapidly growing markets for their products. The latter was important because it gave rise to close links between financial and real exports during this period, especially in the case of the UK. Thanks to the country's industrial pre-eminence, a high proportion of UK foreign investment was used to purchase its exports. To industrialise and develop their economies, capital importing countries needed manufactured goods; and the UK was the leading producer of a wide range of such goods. There was no need, therefore, for official intervention to restrict UK lending abroad, or to ensure that the loans were used mainly to buy UK products. This was happening in any case, stimulating investment and production at home in food processing and export industries. Strong economic complementarity between the UK and the rest of the world guaranteed such an outcome. Consequently, at least before 1900, foreign investment was quite clearly in the country's interest.

In contrast, France and Germany, neither of which had yet reached a level of industrial competitiveness comparable to the UK's, tried to discourage exports of capital (in order to speed up their domestic development) as well as to tie them to orders for their exports. Government efforts to restrict exports of capital were much more in evidence in Germany, which may explain partly why the Germans invested less abroad during the gold standard period than the French (Fishlow 1985, p. 401). However, by 1910 German manufacturers had become so competitive internationally that, unlike their French counterparts, they did not require foreign lending to be tied to their exports.

In addition to the advantages just described, foreign investment were profitable. Most of them brought higher returns than comparable investments at home – appreciably so in the UK case (Edelstein 1982, Davis and Huttenback 1988). This explains why the well-publicised defaults by borrowing countries did not stop the flow of international investment for very long. The receipts from dividends and interest payments were so large in the last part of the period that they were sufficient to finance further investment abroad.

Borrowing countries which used foreign investment productively also derived considerable benefits from it. First, as Tables 3.1 and 3.2 show, in some countries foreign borrowing was responsible for financing a significant proportion of domestic fixed investment (see also Kuznets 1966, chapter 6). Even when this share was not large, capital inflows released some domestic savings for investment in manufacturing and primary activities, thus increasing the countries' capacity to substitute imports and/or expand exports – something that would not have been possible otherwise. Second, direct investment combined inflows of foreign capital with those of technical knowledge and managerial expertise, both of which contributed further to the success of industrialisation in North America and Europe (cf. Wilkins 1989, Millward and Saul 1977). This was less true of direct investment in other parts of the world. There, it went mainly into plantation crops and mining, and was generally of much less benefit to the primary producing than to capital exporting countries.

Finally, as emphasised earlier, no country could have run persistent current account deficits and remained on the gold standard by financing these deficits out of its gold and foreign exchange reserves or, alternatively, by short-term borrowing. Hence, the ability to absorb net imports of goods and services year after year in order to sustain domestic industrialisation had to depend ultimately on the ability to raise long-term loans abroad. In other words, persistent current account deficits could have been financed only by net inflows of long-term capital.

This may seem logical enough, but it is difficult to prove empirically. Balance of payments accounts were not compiled at the time, especially in the form familiar today. Consequently, they are very difficult to construct now from the information

*Table* 3.2   Net capital inflows (+) and outflows (–) as a percentage of gross domestic fixed investment[a]

|           | *1880–90* | *1891–1900* | *1901–10* | *1911–13* |
|-----------|-----------|-------------|-----------|-----------|
| USA       | 5.2       | –1.3        | –1.1      | –0.3      |
| Australia | 50.5      | 22.6        | –8.8      | 10.0      |
| Canada    | n.a.      | n.a.        | 28.9      | 46.2      |
| Italy     | 12.6      | –17.4       | –10.6     | –0.9      |
| Sweden    | 47.0      | 15.2        | 25.1      | –4.9      |
| Norway    | –6.6      | 25.0        | 26.9      | 11.7      |

[a]Additional data for Sweden and Canada, not included in this table, suggest that by far the largest proportion of these flows consisted of long-term investments.
*Source*: Bloomfield (1968).

available. One of the reasons for this is that, even where they exist, data for international capital flows did not distinguish between short-term and long-term lending and borrowing.

One of the notable exceptions is Sweden, and Table 3.3 sets out the results of a rough attempt to construct Sweden's balance of payments during the gold standard period. The most interesting figures in the table are those in columns two and four – showing that Sweden could never have run its persistent current account deficits without continuous, substantial net inflows of long-term capital. Except for the few years just before the First World War, its net flows of short-term capital were very small – exactly the same position as in Canada (Bloomfield 1968), another persistent deficit country for which relevant data exist (see also Viner 1924, Ingram 1957). In fact, thanks to its ability to attract foreign investment on such a scale, Sweden was in the position to finance persistent current account deficits, generate net short-term investment abroad and still run surpluses on its overall balance of payments throughout the period. Not surprisingly, as pointed out in the previous chapter, the country kept increasing its reserves of gold and foreign exchange.

There is little reason to doubt that, if they were available, balance of payments data would reveal a similar financial

102

## European Monetary Union

Table 3.3   Sweden's balance of payments, 1880–1913
(million kroner)

|  | Current balance | Long-term capital[a] | Basic balance | Short-term capital | Overall balance |
|---|---|---|---|---|---|
| 1880–84 | –257 | 256 | –1 | 8 | 7 |
| 1885–89 | –315 | 339 | 24 | –15 | 9 |
| 1890–94 | –144 | 180 | 36 | –21 | 15 |
| 1895–99 | –114 | 145 | 31 | –8 | 23 |
| 1900–04 | –399 | 414 | 15 | 21 | 36 |
| 1905–09 | –417 | 407 | –10 | 51 | 41 |
| 1910–13 | 78 | 112 | 190 | –155 | 35 |

[a]Net inflows = +. Net outflows = –.
Sources: Mitchell (1975) and Bloomfield (1968).

position for other members of 'The Club' which ran current account deficits year after year while continuing to industrialise rapidly. Otherwise, their experience would have differed little from that of Italy and Argentina. Both these countries were forced to leave the gold standard during the 1890s when (because of their policies and financial problems in the late 1880s) they were unable to attract adequate inflows of long-term capital. They readopted the standard at the turn of the century when their position improved dramatically in this respect (cf. Cohen 1967, Ford 1962, Woodruff 1982).

## INTERNATIONAL MIGRATION OF LABOUR

Large-scale international labour mobility was another important factor in sustaining the gold standard arrangements (cf. Thomas 1973, Gould 1979). Around fifty-two million people emigrated from Europe between 1840 and 1930, mainly to North and South America. This was equivalent to 20 per cent of the population of Europe at the beginning of the period (United Nations 1979, p. 1). Another fifty million left China and India, predominantly to work in the tropics (Lewis 1978b, p. 14). Most of this extraordinary movement of people – about

50 per cent of total international migration in the period 1840–1930 – took place between 1880 and 1914. That was equal to slightly over 11 per cent of the increase in world population during the gold standard period (Panić 1988, p. 172). Nothing like this has happened either before or since.

Two factors made international migration on this scale possible. First, there were significant improvements in transport and communications during the period. The improvements made people better informed about other countries and, even more important, reduced sharply the cost of moving even to distant parts of the world (see Woodruff 1982, chapter 6). Consequently, a relatively unfavourable or deteriorating economic (and to a lesser extent social and political) environment at home encouraged people to emigrate to countries where economic conditions and future prospects were more promising. As one would expect, men and women of working age, especially the former, constituted by far the largest proportion of international migrants.

Second, there were vast, virtually empty areas of the world in North and South America, and in Oceania, all rich in minerals and/or agricultural land. Improvements in transport gave the 'new' countries a chance to industrialise by developing their natural wealth and exchanging it for Europe's industrial products. But to do this, they had first to increase their labour force. Consequently, they were more than happy to welcome immigrants – especially those from Europe, many of whom had the skills which were essential for sustained economic development. A number of these countries offered special incentives to encourage international migration, as did the densely populated sending nations in Europe (Kenwood and Lougheed 1983, pp. 63–5).

Table 3.4 shows the extent to which some of the countries featuring most prominently in international migration, either as senders or receivers, participated in the process. In the first group, only the UK and Italy maintained high levels of emigration throughout the period. In both these cases, the levels were sufficiently high to reduce appreciably the growth of domestic

Table 3.4  International migration and growth of population, 1880–1910: selected countries

| | Migration (000s) | | | Migration per decade as % of population at the beginning of decade | | | Population growth per decade as % of population at the beginning of decade | | |
|---|---|---|---|---|---|---|---|---|---|
| | 1880–90 | 1890–1900 | 1900–10 | 1880–90 | 1890–1900 | 1900–10 | 1880–1890 | 1890–1900 | 1900–10 |
| *Sending countries* | | | | | | | | | |
| UK | −1801 | −765 | −1319 | −5.2 | −2.0 | −3.2 | 8.3 | 9.8 | 9.1 |
| Italy | −996 | −1545 | −846 | −3.5 | −4.9 | −2.5 | 7.5 | 6.3 | 9.0 |
| Austria-Hungary | −379 | −683 | −2201 | −1.0 | −1.7 | −4.8 | 9.2 | 10.1 | 8.9 |
| Spain | −251 | −1054 | −964 | −1.5 | −6.0 | −5.2 | 5.5 | 6.1 | 7.2 |
| Germany | −1363 | −604 | −276 | −3.0 | −1.2 | −0.5 | 9.2 | 13.8 | 15.2 |
| Sweden | −329 | −168 | −174 | −7.2 | −3.5 | −3.4 | 4.8 | 7.3 | 7.0 |
| France | −119 | −51 | −53 | −0.3 | −0.1 | −0.1 | 1.8 | 1.6 | 1.6 |
| *Receiving countries* | | | | | | | | | |
| USA | 4492 | 2532 | 5285 | 8.9 | 4.0 | 7.0 | 25.4 | 20.7 | 21.4 |
| Brazil | 449 | 1198 | 622 | 3.8 | 8.4 | 3.5 | 20.9 | 26.7 | 23.5 |
| Argentina | 638 | 320 | 1120 | 25.6 | 9.5 | 24.3 | 35.5 | 36.4 | 43.0 |
| Australia | 383 | 25 | 41 | 16.6 | 0.8 | 1.1 | 40.5 | 18.0 | 19.6 |
| Canada | −205 | −181 | 716 | −4.9 | −3.7 | 13.2 | 11.6 | 11.8 | 34.4 |

*Source:* Green and Urquhart (1976).

population. This was even more true of Spain and Austria-Hungary in the second half of the period, when their emigration accelerated sharply. German emigration, on the other hand, slowed down significantly after 1890; and Sweden's, after halving in the 1890s, remained unchanged until 1914 – continuing, nevertheless, to be fairly large in relation to the growth of its population. In contrast, the rate of emigration from France was negligible throughout the period.

As one would expect, population increased much faster in the receiving countries, mostly by the growth in the indigenous population rather than as a result of immigration. Nevertheless, with the exception of Australia after 1890 and Canada before 1900, immigrants made a far from negligible contribution to the overall increase in population of these countries (cf. Woodruff 1982, pp. 110–11).

As already pointed out, international migration can influence internal (employment and inflation) and external (balance of payments) balances, especially when it consists predominantly of those of working age. To begin with, it helps sending countries to reduce unemployment levels caused either by a sharp decline of certain sectors or by a rapid increase in the working population, or both. Changes of this kind can create serious economic, social and political problems if they are not accompanied by an appropriately fast growth of new industries.

This is precisely what happened in many European countries before 1914. Exceptionally rapid increases in their population during the period (cf. Woodruff 1982, pp. 62–3; Green and Urquhart 1976, p. 218) resulted in diminishing returns on land, forcing people to leave agriculture as it became unable to support them even in times of good harvests. The need for economic restructuring was made even more urgent by two additional developments: improvements in methods of agricultural production which required less labour; and imports of cheap grain from America. The pressure to transfer labour from agriculture into other sectors was particularly strong in the UK where agriculture was completely unprotected, as well as in countries, such as Germany, whose agricultural population was still relatively large. The problem was that in many countries other sectors, such as manufacturing and railways, were not expanding fast enough to absorb surplus population from agriculture. Nor surprisingly, most European emigrants were rural workers and, to a lesser extent, artisans displaced by the growth of manufacturing.

These were the broad trends over the whole period. However, there were important variations around the trends, reflecting economic conditions and the growth of per capita incomes in sending and receiving countries. For instance, Table 3.4 shows that, after declining during the 1890s, emigration from the UK increased sharply in the 1900s as the growth of output and productivity slowed down, unemployment went up and real wages declined. The Italian experience was similar. The number of its emigrants was 55 per cent higher in the 1890s, when the growth of its industrial output came to a standstill (Rostow 1978, pp. 440), than in the 1880s. It almost halved in the 1900s when the country experienced a marked improvement in its economic performance. The table also shows that immigration into the United States and Argentina declined significantly during the 1890s when both these countries experienced considerable economic problems. On the other hand, where the pace of industrialisation was sufficiently fast to expand employment opportunities at home, emigration either slowed down (as in Sweden) or declined sharply (as in Germany). Similarly, emigration from Canada turned into large-scale immigration at the turn of the century as the country entered a period of sustained, rapid industrialisation.

Generally, a modest increase in population means lower demand for goods and services than would have happened otherwise and thus, in conditions in which there is no spare capacity, lower inflation and imports. At the same time, since there is an excess supply of labour, emigration need not affect total output and exports adversely in the short to medium term. The country's current balance of payments also benefits from remittances sent home by the emigrants. This was, for example, an important factor in the Italian economic recovery after 1896 when sizeable remittances from abroad helped balance its current account.

As one would expect, international migration on the scale experienced between 1880 and 1914 had a major effect on investment levels in both sending and receiving countries (see Thomas 1973). For reasons described earlier in this chapter, the required volume of investment in housing, hospitals, schools and other social capital will be influenced significantly by changes in the size of a country's population and by the movement of people from land to towns. Urbanisation, in particular, tends to be highly capital intensive.

Table 3.5 shows that population-related investment (in housing, transport, schools and urban social capital) was higher, as a proportion of their gross national product, in receiving than in sending countries – with the exception of France whose emigration, as already pointed out, was negligible. It is also noticeable that the jump in population-related investment in Germany after 1890 (Table 3.5) coincided with the fall in its rate of emigration (Table 3.4).

The extent to which emigration benefited wages and salaries in sending countries depended on the overall rate of growth of their economies and the improvements in productivity which this generated. On its own, emigration is unlikely to produce marked improvements in this respect unless it gives rise to relative labour scarcity. There is evidence that this is precisely what happened in the Scandinavian countries. The Swedish working population, for example, increased much more slowly than the German and UK labour forces (Phelps Brown and Browne 1968, p. 324). Together with heavy inflows of long-term capital, emigration from the country is judged to have 'made possible the rapid increase in the standard of living in Sweden' (Fleetwood 1947, p. 45). Riis and Thonstad (1989) reach exactly the same conclusion for Norway.

The impact of immigration on receiving countries is, of course, quite different. It increases their labour force and population – expanding the productive potential of the economies

Table 3.5 Population-related investment as a proportion of total domestic output and fixed investment

| | Population-related investment as % of gross national product | | | | Population-related investment as % of total domestic gross fixed investment | | | |
|---|---|---|---|---|---|---|---|---|
| | 1880 | 1890 | 1900 | 1910 | 1880 | 1890 | 1900 | 1910 |
| *Sending countries* | | | | | | | | |
| UK | 4.3 | 3.3 | 5.9 | 3.0 | 52.3 | 46.0 | 56.4 | 45.5 |
| Italy | 2.2 | 1.6 | 2.2 | 1.7 | 22.1 | 18.3 | 18.2 | 11.2 |
| Germany | 4.8 | 6.0 | 6.3 | 6.1 | 59.8 | 48.7 | 42.0 | 43.2 |
| Sweden | 4.8 | 3.4 | 5.3 | 3.7 | 43.7 | 33.2 | 38.3 | 28.1 |
| France | 11.9 | 11.0 | 11.2 | 10.8 | 60.1 | 57.0 | 52.6 | 51.4 |
| *Receiving countries* | | | | | | | | |
| USA | 7.4 | 7.9 | 4.2 | 5.5 | 37.2 | 33.2 | 19.4 | 26.3 |
| Australia | 7.7 | 7.6 | 6.5 | 7.5 | 40.6 | 44.1 | 42.7 | 49.5 |
| Canada | n.a. | 9.2 | 7.5 | 10.8 | n.a. | 58.8 | 56.8 | 42.6 |

n.a. = not available.
*Source:* Green and Urquhart (1976).

as well as the size of the domestic market. At the same time, all this tends to increase domestic demand and imports relative to exports, causing the current balance of payments to deteriorate in the short to medium term. Receiving countries have therefore to increase domestic savings and investment appreciably, both to develop the infrastructure and other social facilities and to expand their industrial base. This is essential if they are to provide employment for their rapidly growing labour force and, in the process, also satisfy the growing demand for goods and services.

Tables 3.1 and 3.5 show that the United States, Canada and Australia – the three most successful receiving countries in terms of their long-term economic performance – devoted a higher proportion of their gross national product throughout this period to domestic fixed investment, both population related and other, than did the sending countries. However, they were able to sustain such high investment levels only by supplementing domestic savings with external borrowing – borrowing which also, as shown in the previous section, enabled persistent deficit countries to balance their current account deficits. Eventually, those receiving countries which successfully developed their productive potential eliminated current account deficits. In the case of the United States, the deficits were turned into equally persistent surpluses.

Finally, diversity of capital and labour movements is as essential as flexibility in monetary and other arrangements if a monetary system is to operate successfully. The important thing is that the flows reflect relative endowments, levels of development and the needs of the countries participating in the system. The experience under the gold standard shows that capital and labour need not always move in the same direction if long-term adjustments are to be accomplished successfully. For instance, of the three surplus countries, the UK and Germany sent both people and capital abroad. In these two cases, higher emigration reduced $I_d$ relative to $S_d$ below what it would have been otherwise. The fact that $S_d > I_d = X > M$ made it possible for them to invest abroad more than they could have done without emigration. France, on the other hand, exported capital but sent very few emigrants and, as shown in the next section, was highly protectionist. Among deficit countries, the United States, Canada and Australia attracted immigrants and foreign investment. The immigrants raised each country's $y_p$ and in the process ensured that $I_d > S_d = M > X$ despite high levels of protection. But Sweden combined a substantial rate of emigration with equally substantial inflows of foreign long-term capital, both of which helped it sustain current account deficits over a long period.

It is very doubtful whether in the absence of such a diversity of behaviour these countries would have been able to realise their economic goals; or whether the international monetary system operating at that time, the gold standard, would have survived for long had their national needs and aspirations been frustrated.


## THE PATTERN OF COMMERCIAL POLICIES

Significant differences in the degree to which members of 'The Club' protected their economies was another factor that made an important contribution to the relative stability and success of the gold standard. It did this by facilitating industrial development within national economies and financial and real transfers of resources between them.

Contrary to widespread belief, barriers to international trade were far from negligible between 1880 and 1914 (cf. Bairoch 1989a and 1989b). To begin with, there were 'natural' obstacles to international specialisation and trade imposed by limitations in the means of transport and, even more so, in the means of communication compared to those common a century later. Hence, tastes, consumption and production were much more localised. On top of this, many countries imposed administrative barriers to trade. These consisted of tariffs, since quantitative restrictions became a favourite policy instrument later, during the First World War. The effectiveness of tariffs can be

*Table* 3.6    Levels of per capita industrialisation, tariffs and foreign investment[a]

| | Per capita industrialisation[b] (UK 1900 = 100) | | Tariff[c] levels on imports of: | | | Foreign investment[d] (billion $ US) |
|---|---|---|---|---|---|---|
| | | | Manufactures | | All goods | |
| | 1880 | 1913 | 1875 | 1913 | 1913 | 1913 |
| United States | 38 | 126 | 38 | 44 | 33 | 3.5 |
| United Kingdom | 87 | 115 | 0 | 0 | 0 | 18.3 |
| Belgium | 43 | 88 | 9–10 | 9 | 6 | }4.3 |
| Switzerland | 39 | 87 | 4–6 | 9 | 7 | |
| Germany | 25 | 85 | 4–6 | 13 | 12 | 5.6 |
| Sweden | 24 | 67 | 3–5 | 20 | 16 | 0.1 |
| France | 28 | 59 | 12–15 | 20 | 18 | 8.7 |
| Canada | 10 | 46 | n.a. | 26 | 18 | (3.0) |
| Denmark | 12 | 33 | n.a. | 14 | 9 | n.a. |
| *Austria* | *15* | *32* | *15–20* | *16* | *17* | n.a. |
| Netherlands | 14 | 28 | 3–5 | 4 | 3 | 1.2 |
| *Italy* | *12* | *26* | *8–10* | *18* | *17* | n.a. |
| *Spain* | *14* | *22* | *15–20* | *41* | *33* | *(0.7)* |
| *Russia* | *10* | *20* | *15–20* | *84* | n.a. | *(3.2)* |
| *Japan* | *9* | *20* | *5* | *30* | n.a. | *(1.0)* |
| *Argentina* | n.a. | n.a. | n.a. | *28* | *26* | *(3.0)* |

[a]Countries which were not permanent members of 'The Club' are shown in italics. [b]Three-year averages. [c] Weighted average of import duties. [d] Figures in brackets show estimates of the combined value of UK, French and German investment in these countries.
*Sources*: Per capita industrialisation – Bairoch (1982); tariffs – Bairoch (1989a) and League of Nations (1927); foreign investment – Woytinsky and Woytinsky (1955) and Woodruff (1982).

judged from the fact that this has been the only time since the 1820s, apart from the period 1914–50, when world industrial production increased faster than world trade – indicating international disintegration in this particular area of economic activity (cf. Panić 1988, chapter 9).

Table 3.6 shows average levels of import duty (a) on all commodities and (b) on manufactured goods only, both expressed as a percentage of the value of total imports in each category. The important thing to notice is that they varied a good deal between countries at the beginning of the period and even more so just before the First World War. In the case of manufactured imports, the *ad valorem* duties ranged in 1875 from zero in the UK to about 20 per cent in several countries – with the US duties exceptionally high at 38 per cent. However, by 1913 the range had widened appreciably: from zero in the UK to over 40 per cent in the United States and Spain and over 80 per cent in Russia.

Thus the changes in protection levels which took place during the period were far from uniform. The differences are apparent even among the countries in which the pace of industrialisation was exceptionally fast. Duties were increased sharply in Sweden and Germany, remained very high in the United States and declined slightly in Denmark. Moreover, the increases were not confined to any particular group. They took place in most members of 'The Club', in latecomers (Russia and Japan) and in countries, such as Spain, which never went on the gold standard. Some of them were already highly industrialised, others in the early phases of economic development. There was, obviously, no pressure on sovereign nation states during the classical gold standard to harmonise their commercial policies. Even membership of 'The Club' was not conditional on such harmonisation.

Nevertheless, the variations in protection levels which existed during the gold standard period were neither capricious nor random. Table 3.6 reveals an important pattern: tariffs tended to be high in countries with relatively low levels of industrialisation and low at the other end of the scale. There were, of course, some conspicuous exceptions, notably the United States and the Netherlands.

In the US case, one of the reasons for this was probably that it had acquired only recently – during a relatively short period of extremely rapid industrialisation – its position of industrial pre-eminence. Furthermore, it was a large, basically self-sufficient economy which had no need to liberalise its trade in order to encourage other countries to do the same, and thus expand its exports. These were after all of marginal importance to the economy, accounting in 1913 for only 6 per cent of its GDP (Maddison 1989, p. 143). As for the Netherlands, despite its low level of industrialisation per capita, the country enjoyed one of the highest incomes per head in the world (see Chapter 1). Moreover, it had played a pioneering role in the Commercial Revolution which preceded the Industrial Revolution. External trade was of vital importance to its economy.

In general, as Table 3.6 shows, countries at higher levels of industrialisation pursued much more liberal commercial policies during the period than countries in the early stages of industrial development. (See also Panić 1988 and 1990.) The inverse relationship between the levels of industrialisation and protection in fact played an important role not just in the development of individual economies but of the international economy as a whole. In doing this, it made a significant contribution to the relatively smooth working of the international gold standard.

To begin with, such differentiation of commercial policies enabled the then 'newly industrialising countries' to reduce unnecessary imports and thus conserve their holdings of gold and foreign exchange to meet more pressing needs. That made the size of their current account deficits – and the financing of these deficits – more manageable.

They were helped in this also by the attitude of the highly industrialised economies, most of which ran current account surpluses during the gold standard period. As Table 3.6 shows, they invested heavily abroad. Moreover, with the exception of France, all these countries (the United Kingdom, Belgium, Switzerland, the Netherlands, and to a lesser extent, Germany) were either committed to free trade or pursued relatively liberal trade policies. This gave less industrialised countries, running chronic current account deficits, relatively easy access to their most important foreign markets. In other words, with a few exceptions, the most industrialised countries allowed almost free entry into their markets while at the same time tolerating restrictions on their exports by less industrialised, deficit countries. That was, of course, particularly true of the most important creditor country: the United Kingdom.

In addition, the differentiation of commercial policies enabled latecomers to develop new industries – especially those that could become viable only by exploiting economies of large-scale production – by protecting them until they were ready to compete against established foreign producers. This became an important aspect of economic policy during the gold standard period, as many industries in this category (such as chemicals, steel and engineering) were developed at that time.

Finally, differences in national trade policies had the effect of making the contraction of the declining sectors, such as European agriculture, more manageable – avoiding unsustainable social costs that would have been incurred by persistent, heavy unemployment. However, thanks to large-scale emigration, it was unnecessary to impose high tariffs for this purpose.

An important aspect of the differences in national trade policies which emerged during the gold standard period is that, like international investment and migration, they were the outcome of largely uncoordinated decisions by individual countries in pursuit of self interest, rather than a result of elaborate international negotiations designed to impose a particular, 'optimum', pattern of trading arrangements. Yet it would be highly misleading to interpret this as an indication that, left to themselves, 'market forces' will always produce a similar outcome. The main reason for this, as already emphasised, is that the arrangements which evolved between 1880 and 1914 among a relatively small number of countries were a consequence of an extraordinary complementarity of resource endowments of the most important members of the international system.

Table 3.7 provides another illustration of this. It compares certain characteristics of the six leading European capital-exporting (surplus) economies with those of the United States, which by 1914 had become the largest and most industrialised economy in the world – beginning to play the role of a major international investor. Together, the six economies were roughly of the same size as the US economy. However, individually, they were much smaller and therefore much less self

*Table* 3.7   Selected characteristics of the leading capital-exporting
countries in 1913

|  | Six European countries[a] | United States |
|---|---|---|
| *Percentage shares* | | |
| *in world* | | |
| GDP | 23.1 | 25.7 |
| Manufacturing output[b] | 37.2 | 32.0 |
| Foreign investment | 90.7 | 8.3 |
| Imports of goods | 46.7 | 9.8 |
| Exports of goods | 41.7  (56.6) | 12.6  (11.0) |
| *Levels[c] of* | | |
| Per capita industrialisation | | |
| (UK 1900 = 100) | 92 | 126 |
| Tariffs – manufactures | 8 | 44 |
|     – all goods | 7 | 33 |

[a]United Kingdom, France, Germany, Belgium, Switzerland and the Netherlands. [b]Excluding the Netherlands whose share in world manufacturing output is not available. [c]Weighted averages.
*Sources*: As in Table 3.6 except for: shares in world GDP and export shares shown in brackets which were calculated from Maddison (1989); and shares of export and imports of goods which were taken from Maddison (1962).

sufficient than the United States. International specialisation and trade were, therefore, of critical importance for their economic development. This explains why, as a group, they were much more prominent in the world economy both as investors and traders; and why their tariff levels were so much lower than those imposed by the Americans. The highly advanced European economies pursued liberal trade policies because it was in their interest to do so.

Fortunately, this also happened to be of great importance for the viability of the gold standard, because it enable capital importing countries – predominantly members of 'The Club' – to expand their merchandise exports, thus earning foreign exchange with which to service and repay their debts. Hence, by attracting long-term foreign investment, they were able to industrialise their economies and finance persistent current account deficits; and by being able to service and repay foreign loans regularly they were in a position to attract more such loans until eventually many of them achieved a sufficiently high level of industrialisation to become net international lenders.

The international economic system worked smoothly, in fact, so long as the six countries played a dominant role in the world economy. When, after the First World War, the centre of economic influence switched to the United States it proved impossible for the 'market forces' to rebuild 'automatically' the complex economic order which had existed before 1914. The new dominant economy was so large and so self-sufficient that it could sustain a high level of industrialisation and income per head by continuing with autarchic policies of the kind indicated in Table 3.7. This made an orderly transfer of financial and real resources between surplus and deficit countries impossible. The result was the disintegration of the world economy at the beginning of the 1930s, the Great Depression (Kindleberger 1973, Panić 1988) and the collapse, after only a few years, of the interwar attempt to recreate the classical gold standard (Nurkse 1944).

## CONCLUSIONS

The preceding sections have provided answers to a number of questions raised in Chapter 2. The behaviour of both surplus and deficit countries – almost incomprehensible within the classical/neoclassical framework – is relatively simple to understand when factor movements and variations in trade policies are included in the analysis. Obviously, important economic adjustments took place during the period, especially among members of 'The Club'. But, as pointed out in the previous chapter, these adjustments were of a long-term nature leading to significant improvements in economic welfare in the countries concerned rather than to costly sacrifices in income and/or employment of the kind predicted by the traditional models.

The most remarkable aspect of the classical gold standard, therefore, is not the willingness of countries at different levels of industrialisation to observe its very strict rules but, rather, the developments which made it possible for these economies to adhere to the rules over such a long period. These developments, in turn, were the outcome of a number of extremely unusual conditions which promoted the establishment of a network of international financial and other arrangements. It is these arrangements that facilitated the extraordinary transfers of resources between countries, making it possible for a relatively small number of them to operate the gold standard for several decades. Consequently, each country was able to reconcile the pursuit of its national interest with the membership of an international monetary union. Although they themselves do not seem to have been aware of this, that is the most important lesson that those responsible for 'real' and financial achievements during the classical gold standard have passed on to posterity.

# 4 Lessons from the Gold Standard Experience

It is clear from the preceding chapters that, although it was never defined in those terms, the classical gold standard combined all the basic characteristics of a quasi monetary union. Capital, in both the short and the long term, moved freely between countries. The same was also true of labour. The exchange rates of countries which adopted the standard were 'irrevocably' fixed to each other within very narrow margins where they were expected to remain indefinitely. There were no provisions for exchange rates to be changed under any circumstances, no matter how 'exceptional'. This meant that, in principle, external balances had to take precedence over internal ones irrespective of losses in output, employment and income that such a commitment involved. A country with serious adjustment problems and unwilling to tolerate such losses for long had either to find a way of reconciling the two balances without sacrificing economic welfare or abandon the standard. There was no other alternative.

Hence, although all members of 'The Club' resorted to various devices intended to make the rigid link between gold reserves and money supply a little more flexible – the freedom that this allowed in the pursuit of national monetary policy was too small to have a significant impact on the 'real' side of their economies. Moreover, there was quite simply no way of escaping the fact that the moment a country tied its currency to gold it also made its monetary policy dependent on the policies of the other countries operating the system. Governments could have had no illusions, therefore, about the effect that a decision to adopt the standard would have on their national monetary independence.

Gold itself, of course, had little to do with this. Exactly the same rules that applied under the gold standard would have had to be observed under any monetary system in which a number of countries similarly employed either a commodity or a currency as their common unit of account.

The other important aspect of the 'gold standard rules' is that, in principle, the difference between those imposed under quasi and under complete monetary union is one of degree rather than kind. The scope for an independent national monetary policy under a system of fixed exchange rates is, as already pointed out, too small compared to that under a complete monetary union to produce a material difference in a country's economic performance.

The one difference between the two monetary systems that does matter is the ability to leave the union. As emphasised in the Introduction, this is relatively easy so long as countries maintain their national currencies and central banks. The experience under the gold standard shows that no matter how much a country's commitment to a system of fixed exchange rates may seem to be firm and irrevocable, the authorities will not hesitate to abandon it if serious adjustment problems threaten to result in a lasting loss in economic welfare and/or in the political influence of its powerful interest groups. This is obviously far from easy if they have to start by creating a separate currency and central bank. Apart from the legal and technical complexities that this involves, the widespread suspicion and lack of confidence that would greet the new national monetary system – and the damage that this could do to the economy – might take a long time to overcome.

These are all important policy issues. However, an analysis of the advantages and disadvantages of a monetary union which is restricted to its monetary aspects is justified only if it can be shown that, *ceteris paribus*, they make a fundamental difference to economic welfare of member countries. In fact, there is no conclusive empirical evidence that exchange rate instability, on its own, tends either to reverse the process of international economic integration or to alter significantly the ability of individual countries to reconcile their internal and

external balances (IMF 1984, Bank of England 1984). These
have always been influenced by a host of complex economic,
social and political factors which, in turn, affect the functioning
– even the survival – of a monetary system. It is for this reason
that, as the gold standard experience shows, the economic
performance of the countries which comprise a monetary union
is at least as important in judging its success and viability as the
performance of the financial system itself. As a result, *both*
have to be taken into account.

\* \* \*

One of the most obvious lessons from the gold standard
experience is that it is increases in international specialisation
and trade – in other words in economic links between countries
– that sooner or later create the need for a single unit of
account, either a commodity standard or a common currency.
Even though uncertainties about future costs and prices in any
one currency in terms of other currencies may not reduce
significantly the volume of international trade, they will affect
economic welfare adversely by making a rational, efficient
allocation of productive resources progressively more difficult.
Monetary diversity, with the risk that independently determined policies will amplify exchange rate volatility, thus
becomes increasingly incompatible in a dynamic international
economy with an efficient use of resources within the continuously rising levels of integration and interdependence.
(See, for instance, EC Commission 1990a). Not surprisingly,
the triumph of the gold over the silver standard in the
nineteenth century *followed* early stages of the Industrial Revolution in the countries which adopted it.

\* \* \*

There are two reasons why under these conditions the commodity or currency chosen to serve as 'the anchor' of an
international monetary union will be the one which is most

compatible with the objective of price stability – ensuring that in credit (unlike metallic) monetary systems 'good' money drives out its 'bad' counterpart.

First, the national and international division of labour increases both social and individual wealth; and it will be the natural desire of wealth holders to protect the value of their assets against rising prices. Moreover, they will be in a position to do something about this, as those who own or manage wealth will enjoy considerable social standing and political influence in their countries. After all, long-term improvements in economic welfare, which are widely desired, depend on their actions concerning the allocation and management of productive resources.

Second, these actions will be easier to carry out successfully if both domestic and international costs and prices are stable and expected to remain so. It is obviously easier to plan future investment and output under these conditions than if the variables that determine profits fluctuate widely. As inflation rates tend to be inversely related to income and efficiency levels (cf. Panić 1976 and 1978), it is either the standard or the currency of the dominant economy that will become the unit of account within a monetary union. This tendency will be reinforced by the fact that the country will account for a large share of global or regional output, trade, savings and international investment. Other countries within the union will, therefore, be anxious to secure easy access to its market for goods, finance, and technical and organisational skills. For all these reasons, the dominant economy is bound to exercise a major influence in the formation and organisation of a monetary union. More accurately, the institutional framework of such a union will reflect the preferences of the powerful interest groups which control the dominant economy.

This, of course, explains why in the nineteenth century the monetary standard and currency of the dominant economy at the time, that of the United Kingdom, assumed such importance in international trade and finance.

* * *

The choice of a common unit of account is important also because it determines the institutional framework responsible for the monetary policy of the union.

An international monetary union requires a unified institutional structure if it is to perform its role of facilitating specialisation and trade between countries. In practice, this means that the system will be run in one of the two ways, depending on the type of union. In the case of a quasi union it will be managed *de facto* (though not *de jure*) by the central bank and financial institutions of the dominant country. A complete monetary union, on the other hand, will be run by a supranational central bank operating through transnational financial institutions, with those from the dominant country in the forefront because of the relatively large volume of savings generated on its territory.

In either case, the subordination of national monetary systems either to that of the dominant economy or to that of a supranational institution modelled on it is likely to be easier under a commodity standard than under an inconvertible currency one.

Provided that there are no controls on international capital flows, the institutional arrangements of a quasi union come into effect the moment a number of countries choose a particular commodity to act as the single unit of account within their economies. For reasons explained in Chapter 1, this will automatically link their currencies and monetary policies to each other; and to the extent that an economy within the union is larger than the rest its institutions and policies will, also automatically, assume key roles in the union. No international negotiations are needed to establish this and thus highlight the fact that in joining the union each country is giving up part of its national sovereignty. Even the fixing of exchange rates appears to be nothing more than the byproduct of a purely national decision to link the value of its currency to a clearly specified quantity of a commodity. The *illusion* of national monetary independence is therefore preserved. That was certainly the case under the gold standard, despite the fact that monetary policies of members of 'The Club' were largely determined by actions of a few national central banks, especially the Bank of England.

The establishment of a complete union inevitably shatters this illusion. Nevertheless, the dominant country's view of how such a system should operate can again be imposed indirectly by ensuring that the supranational monetary authority accepts its commodity standard. This should be relatively easy to achieve if a complete union replaces a system of rigidly fixed exchange rates, as all countries forming it will already be on the same commodity standard as the dominant economy. The rules guiding the behaviour of the common central bank will thus appear to be no different from those which were originally in operation in *all* member countries of the newly formed union.

Differences of this kind may not mean much in practice. Nevertheless, they are important in the sense that implicitly they reconcile the requirements of greater international economic integration with those of national political sensibilities which play a key role in the *creation* of monetary unions.

At the same time, as emphasised earlier in this book, the great disadvantage of all commodity standards is that, ultimately, the money supply of the countries which operate them is determined not by those responsible for their economic policy but by the actions of those who produce the commodity. Given the close relationship between economic success, social harmony and political stability, it is perfectly understandable that no government would now seriously contemplate fixing the value of its currency to a particular commodity. But this does mean that it is more difficult to create an international monetary union under these conditions without protracted, well-publicised negotiations; and these are most likely to reach a successful conclusion if they take into account those factors which are of special concern to powerful economic interests in *all* the countries concerned.

\* \* \*

The institutional form of a monetary union is important because it defines the policy rules to be followed by the authorities.

Provided that currencies are freely convertible and that central banks make no attempt to sterilise international capital flows, the stabilisation process in a system of fixed exchange rates will operate according to the rules traditionally associated with the gold standard. A country whose monetary policy is more expansionary than the policies pursued by other members of the union will be forced (by its limited reserves and capital outflows) to reverse it. Capital inflows and monetary expansion should, in theory, ensure that underutilised capacity is eliminated in the surplus country.

In fact, a quasi monetary union tends to be asymmetric, in the sense that the pressure to pursue stabilisation policies does not apply equally to deficit and surplus countries. For reasons described above (see also Chapter 2) a deficit country has no alternative but to eliminate excess demand. A surplus country, on the other hand, can choose any or all of the following options: it can expand economic activity; it can sterilise capital inflows by accumulating reserves and thus maintain, even increase further, the level of its underutilised resources; and it can lend to other countries – in each case maintaining its exchange rate fixed.

Monetary policy in a complete union is, of course, determined by the supranational central bank. If it is a regional union, the policy stance adopted by the bank will depend on whether the union as a whole is in surplus or deficit with the rest of the world; and, as in the case of a single country within a quasi union, that will also influence the urgency with which the union has to pursue the appropriate stabilisation policy. Moreover, although the same policy will be applied to the whole union, its impact will be felt equally by member countries only if all of them are experiencing excess demand or underutilised capacity to a similar extent. Otherwise, the effect of both expansionary and contractionary policies will be much greater in some parts of the union than in others.

The institutional framework of a monetary union may, in fact, have important implications for the overall stance of stabilisation policy within the union. Broadly speaking, it is likely to be more deflationary in a quasi than in a complete union, for the simple reason that surplus countries will have much more influence on economic policy in the former where it will still be decided at the national level. If they persist with tight monetary policies even when their economies operate with unused resources and, at the same time, refuse to extend credit to deficit countries, the latter will have no alternative but to maintain restrictive policies. *Ceteris paribus*, this is less likely to be the case in a complete union when monetary policy has to be determined collectively. The difference may be significant if the countries and regions which normally experience much more serious unemployment problems in the course of a recession have an important say in formulating policy.

* * *

The asymmetries and inequalities are even more pronounced if the union consists of countries with serious structural disequilibria which require them to undertake long-term adjustments. The problem arises when some countries can achieve full employment in the short run without high inflation and external imbalances while others can reconcile full employment and low inflation only with current account deficits. Outside a monetary union, a country in the second group would be able, at least in theory, to achieve external balance by devaluing its currency, thus providing protection and subsidies to all its tradeable sectors – competitive and uncompetitive. In other words, it could adopt a policy that would suit its national interests irrespective of the effect that this might have on other countries. That, of course, is precisely something no country is allowed to do within a monetary union, quasi or complete.

Consequently, if structural deficit countries join a quasi union they can achieve the desired adjustment in three ways – two of which depend critically on the cooperation of other members. First, they can reduce their income either in absolute terms or relative to those of other countries. This will diminish their capacity to import while at the same time releasing productive resources for exports. If they adopt this strategy, deficits on their current balance of payments will disappear, but at the expense of growing income inequalities within the union. The danger inherent in this is that, unless the process is reversed, there will be growing internal pressure in such countries to leave the union; and, as the gold standard experience shows, sovereign states which find themselves in this position will do so.

Second, deficit countries can borrow long term from those running persistent current account surpluses. Provided that they can do this on a scale sufficient to achieve their economic objectives, there will be no reason to leave the union. In fact, if international capital flows and transfers of resources are such that they enable deficit countries to raise their efficiency and income levels relative to those enjoyed by leading members of the union, the need for monetary integration will be strengthened as a result of much greater division of labour and, consequently, much greater economic interdependence between member countries.

Third, similar results can also be achieved through adequate emigration of labour from deficit to surplus countries.

Exactly the same adjustment options will also be available in a complete union. The only difference is that, as all countries use the same currency, balance of payments imbalances now assume the form of financial surpluses of firms, individuals and governments in successful, prosperous parts of the union and financial deficits in its less successful areas (cf. Hartland 1949). The future of the union depends, therefore, on maintaining an adequate transfer of resources, private and official, from the former to the latter (see ibid).

As shown in the previous chapter, capital and labour movements were of critical importance in enabling members of 'The Club' to stay on the gold standard throughout its existence. That is one of the most important lessons to emerge from international economic history of the pre-1914 period.

Equally important, the experience should not be interpreted as meaning that similar factor movements can take place within any monetary union so long as there are no barriers to their mobility. Between 1880 and 1914 these movements made a significant contribution to the adjustment process in a relatively small number of economies – all of which were complementary to an extent that is unlikely ever to be repeated again. Nevertheless, even under these conditions, it was necessary for governments to play a major role in providing incentives for capital and labour to move in the desired direction. This suggests that governmental attitudes and policies are likely to be of even more strategic importance in less favourable circumstances, both in facilitating factor movements and in arranging official transfers from surplus to deficit countries and regions.

* * *

The stabilisation and adjustment rules imposed by a monetary union mean that great care should be taken in deciding its membership, for this will ultimately determine the viability of the whole enterprise. As emphasised in the preceding chapters, not all countries are equally able to reconcile internal and external balances under these rules.

Not surprisingly, the question of what constitutes an 'optimum currency area' – in other words, the optimum membership of a quasi monetary union – has received a good deal of attention. There seems to be general agreement among economists that the union should consist of countries which are highly integrated and, as a group, largely self-sufficient both economically (McKinnon 1963, Kenen 1969) and financially (Ingram 1973, Scitovsky 1958). A high level of international integration and interdependence reduces the effectiveness of exchange rates in the adjustment process. The act of fixing the rates (even of adopting a single currency) does not, therefore, deprive the countries concerned of an effective policy instrument. A high level of intra-group self-sufficiency reduces the impact of external shocks in member countries and thus the need for any one of them to resort to exchange rate changes in order to deal with the adjustment problems caused by such shocks.

However, as some economists have pointed out (Haberler 1970, Fleming 1971), members of a monetary union have to have something else in common: inflation rates and policy preferences. If these differ significantly, it becomes virtually impossible to coordinate national monetary policies and thus to sustain the union. As the coordination of policies is easiest to achieve among countries at a similar level of efficiency and incomes (Panić 1988), the implication is that a monetary union should consist of such countries. To the extent that it does not, a high degree of capital and labour mobility – provided that the factors move in the right direction – is essential if member countries are to adjust without welfare losses (Mundell 1961).

In retrospect, 'The Club' satisfied these conditions despite the fact that no one made a conscious effort to ensure that it did so. The countries were highly interdependent, represented a virtually closed economic system (not least because they had direct control over large areas of the world outside 'The Club'), allowed an extraordinary degree of capital and labour mobility which, in turn, made it relatively easy for them to coordinate macroeconomic policies even when their efficiency and income levels were markedly different. The adjustment problems were also made more manageable in the short term by considerable differences in national trade policies.

\* \* \*

Given that the criteria described above will be satisfied at any one time by a relatively small number of countries, the greater the diversity of economies that wish to join a monetary union the less rigid should be its 'entry' and 'exit' conditions.

A country should enter such a union – especially a complete one – only when it is ready and able to follow the adjustment and stabilisation rules without having to sacrifice income and employment. Equally, it should be able to leave it if this becomes impossible or if, on joining the union, it discovers that this was a costly mistake. The latter provision is important because some countries may take such a step for reasons of national 'prestige' rather than on the basis of a rational assessment of its economic costs and benefits. (See, for example, Yeager 1984 for a few examples of such considerations in the nineteenth century.)

For all these reasons, countries should not contemplate a complete union – with the problems which it creates for anyone wishing to leave it – until their differences in economic performance are so small, or compensatory factor movements so large, that both absolute and relative gains in economic welfare clearly outweigh any benefits that could be derived outside it.

Although the governments of the countries concerned never even considered the wisdom of flexible 'membership', this is in effect what happened during the classical gold standard. Moreover, they made no deliberate attempt to harmonise their policies, even less to turn 'The Club' into an economic union. Monetary uniformity imposed by the standard was reconciled with a variety of economic policy instruments, adopted by each country according to its specific needs and objectives.

* * *

Finally, the classical gold standard had an important advantage over purely regional monetary unions. Although, strictly speaking, it was not a global monetary system, it did include all the most advanced economies of the time. Moreover, some of them exercised direct political and economic control over numerous other nations and countries. As a result, members of 'The Club' formed an effective optimum policy area (see Panić 1988). The monetary and other policies that affected their economies were those pursued by other – particularly surplus – insiders. Weak economies outside 'the union' responded to policies initiated by powerful economies within it. They had little influence on them.

It is for this reason that the relationship of an international monetary union with other comparable systems has been ignored in this book. (See, however, Panić 1988, chapter 16, for an analysis of the problems that this might create.) Moreover, the absence of a serious competitor to the classical gold standard does not seriously diminish the relevance of its experience to the countries contemplating the creation of a European Monetary Union. The size, diversity and degree of economic interdependence of the EC countries make it virtually certain that the success and viability of a monetary union between them will be determined chiefly by the economic organisation and policies that they adopt.

# 5 Postscript: A Comparison of EC and Gold Standard Countries

As pointed out in the Introduction, there are a number of important similarities between the monetary union that the European Community intends to create in the late 1990s and the quasi monetary union operated by countries which adopted the classical gold standard. At the same time, there are also important differences. Many of the steps either taken or planned by the European Community go well beyond anything attempted under the gold standard.

For instance, unlike members of the EC, no country on the gold standard was either expected or required to harmonise its policies with those of other countries. To the extent that it had to do this in the monetary sphere, such harmonisation was the automatic outcome of adopting the gold standard. Even this did not completely eliminate noticeable differences in the conduct of monetary policy – though, of course, no central bank could adopt a policy stance which differed significantly from those taken by its foreign counterparts. For reasons analysed in the preceding chapters, the system would never have survived for as long as it did had countries on the gold standard failed to observe strictly the discipline that the monetary interdependence imposed on them.

At the same time, there were often considerable differences in other areas of national economic management, notably in trade policy. As shown in Chapter 3, some countries (France, Canada and especially the United States) maintained fairly high tariff levels on their imports throughout the gold standard period. Others (the Netherlands, Switzerland and particularly the United Kingdom) pursued a policy of free trade.

In other words, a country on the classical gold standard was not required by international treaties to abolish all barriers on trade with other members of the *de facto* monetary union. It was under even less obligation to harmonise indirect taxes or technical, health and other standards. Hence, although their monetary policies were highly interdependent, countries on the gold standard still maintained a considerable degree of independence in the pursuit of their national economic and social objectives. The standard, unlike the EC, never atttempted to be an economic union. In fact, the countries concerned showed no desire to create a complete monetary union either.

Nevertheless, despite various protective devices to which weaker members of 'The Club' resorted, the existing disparities in efficiency and income levels required massive resource transfers to support what was a rather exacting *quasi* monetary union. This raises a question of considerable importance for the long-term viability and success of the European Community: how do disparities in levels of industrialisation and income among EC countries, their economic performance and their resource transfers compare with those of members of 'The Club'?

This chapter analyses a number of statistical indicators, available for both periods, to produce some tentative comparisons. The comparisons cannot be regarded as anything other than tentative given that the data are not always strictly comparable and that they suffer from various shortcomings (see the original sources for this). This is particularly true of the statistics for the period before 1914. Consequently, it would be unwise to attach much importance to small differences.

## INTERNATIONAL DIFFERENCES IN PER CAPITA LEVELS OF INDUSTRIALISATION AND INCOME

Chapter 1 included an analysis of industrialisation and income levels among the gold standard countries. Table 5.1 provides similar information for members of the European Community.

*Table* 5.1   Per capita levels of industrialisation and income in EC countries

| | Industrialisation[a] (UK 1900 = 100) | GDP ($ at 1985 prices) | |
|---|---|---|---|
| | 1980 | 1980 | 1988 |
| Luxembourg | n.a. | 11 258 | 13 933 |
| West Germany | 395 | 11 016 | 12 604 |
| France | 277 | 11 166 | 12 190 |
| Denmark | 356 | 10 312 | 12 089 |
| UK | 325 | 9 681 | 11 982 |
| Italy | 231 | 10 015 | 11 741 |
| Belguim | 316 | 10 529 | 11 495 |
| Netherlands | 245 | 10 585 | 11 468 |
| Spain | 159 | 6 525 | 7 406 |
| Ireland | 147 | 6 189 | 6 239 |
| Greece | 114 | 5 494 | 5 857 |
| Portugal | 130 | 4 507 | 5 321 |

[a]Three-year averages. 1980 is the last year for which comparable indices of industrialisation are available for all these countries.
*Sources*: Industrialisation – Bairoch (1982). GDP – Summers and Heston (1988 and 1991).

The most striking fact about these figures is the apparent gulf which exists between the top eight countries in the table and the four so-called 'Southern' members: Spain, Ireland, Greece and Portugal. The lowest per capita levels of industrialisation (Italy) and income (the Netherlands) among the eight leading economies are still considerably higher (by 45 and 55 per cent respectively) than those in Spain, economically the most advanced of the remaining four members. The division appears to be much more pronounced than that which existed between the gold standard countries (see Table 1.1).

However, on closer inspection, a comparison of differences in efficiency and income levels within 'The Club' and the EC produces results which are much less clear cut. According to Table 5.2, levels of industrialisation (measured as the volume of industrial output per head) are a good deal less unequal in the Community than in 'The Club' – though the rather wide differences prevailing in 1880 were reduced significantly by

*Table* 5.2   Disparities in per capita levels of industrialisation and income: the gold standard and EC countries

| | Gold standard | | European Community | |
|---|---|---|---|---|
| | *1880* | *1913* | *1980* | *1988* |
| *Industrialisation*[a] | | | | |
| (UK 1900 = 100) | | | | |
| Mean | 29 | 66 | 245 | n.a. |
| Standard deviation | 21 | 35 | 97 | n.a. |
| Coefficient of | | | | |
| variation (%) | *72.4* | *53.0* | *39.6* | n.a. |
| *Ratios (means)* | | | | |
| Top 3/bottom 3 countries | *4.67*[b] | *4.07*[c] | *2.76*[d] | *n.a.* |
| *GNP or GDP* | | | | |
| ($ at constant prices) | | | | |
| Mean | 514 | 846 | 8 940 | 10 194 |
| Standard deviation | 143 | 234 | 2 512 | 3 099 |
| Coefficient of | | | | |
| variation (%) | *27.8* | *27.6* | *28.1* | *30.4* |
| *Ratios (means)* | | | | |
| Top 3/bottom 3 countries | *1.94*[e] | *1.95*[f] | *2.06*[g] | *2.22*[g] |

[a]Excluding Luxembourg, for which indices of industrialisation are not available. [b]UK, Belgium and Switzerland vs. Canada, Denmark and the Netherlands. [c]USA, UK and Belgium vs. Finland, the Netherlands and Norway. [d]West Germany, Denmark and UK vs. Greece, Portugal and Ireland. [e]USA, UK and Canada vs. Finland, Norway and Sweden. [f]USA, Canada and UK vs. Finland, Norway and France. [g]Luxembourg, West Germany and France vs. Portugal, Greece and Ireland.
*Sources*: Tables 1.1 and 5.1.

1913. The disparities in income levels, on the other hand, appear to be surprisingly similar. The only noticeable dissimilarity is that dispersions around the mean income remain unchanged between 1880 and 1913, in contrast to a slight increase among members of the Community during the 1980s.

On the whole, the data set out in Tables 5.1 and 5.2 could be interpreted as providing some encouragement to those who would like to speed up the creation of a full monetary union of the kind approved at the Maastricht Summit. Why should the observed differences in efficiency and income levels pose a threat to the European monetary union when, apparently, they did not prevent the classical gold standard from functioning successfully over such a long period?

One of the problems in drawing confidently conclusions of this kind is that the very broad national averages, such as those analysed above, may hide considerable regional differences. Fortunately, these can be taken into account for the more recent period, as relevant data are available for EC countries.

Table 5.3 sets out the dispersion of the Community's regions according to their income per head relative to the EC average. For instance, it shows that there are two regions (one in West Germany and the other in the Netherlands) with incomes over 80 per cent above the mean for the Community as a whole. At the other extreme, there are eight regions – all but one in Greece and Portugal – whose average incomes are less than half the EC average. In general, as one would expect, regional data of income per head confirm the conclusion reached from the aggregate national data. With the exception of a small region in Spain, all the regions with per capita income above the Community average are to be found in the top eight countries.

Not surprisingly, regional differences in income per head within the Community as a whole are much greater than those that exist in individual countries. This can be seen from Table 5.4. The ratios of the highest to the lowest regional income vary within countries, from 1.4 in Denmark to 2.7 in the Netherlands. In contrast, comparing the highest regional income in the EC with the lowest for each member country produces much greater variations: from 1.5 for Luxembourg to 4.4 for Portugal and 4.6 for Greece. The comparable ratios for Spain (3.7) and Ireland (2.8) are lower than the last two, though they also exceed the highest national ratio (2.7 in the Netherlands). Among the eight high income countries this is true only of Italy (3.1). In the other seven cases, the ratios between the Community's highest and the national lowest regional income per head are well within the differences tolerated in individual countries.

If one takes this as a very rough indication of the ratio that the Community would have to aim for in the long run, to avoid

Table 5.3  Dispersion of regional income per capita in the European Community (number of regions and, in brackets, their % share of each country's population. EC average GDP per capita = 100)

| Member countries and their population (EC = 100) | 180 | 170 | 160 | 150 | 140 | 130 | 120 | 110 | 100 | 90 | 80 | 70 | 60 | 50 | 40 |
|---|---|---|---|---|---|---|---|---|---|---|---|---|---|---|---|
| Luxembourg (0.1) | | | | | | | 1 (100.0) | | | | | | | | |
| West Germany (18.9) | 1 (2.6) | | | | 2 (6.3) | 2 (11.6) | 4 (17.9) | 3 (12.6) | 7 (22.1) | 10 (24.3) | 1 (0.5) | 1 (2.1) | | | |
| France (17.2) | | | 1 (18.6) | | | | | 2 (5.8) | 4 (20.3) | 6 (24.4) | 8 (30.3) | 1 (0.6) | | | |
| Denmark (1.6) | | | | | | 1 (31.2) | | | 1 (56.2) | 1 (12.6) | | | | | |
| UK (17.6) | | | 1 (11.9) | | | | 2 (2.3) | 5 (13.6) | 10 (30.7) | 7 (18.8) | 10 (22.7) | | | | |
| Italy (17.7) | | | | | | 2 (15.2) | 1 (6.8) | 7 (37.4) | 1 (2.2) | 1 (1.7) | 1 (2.2) | 4 (19.2) | 2 (11.3) | 1 (4.0) | |
| Belgium (3.0) | | | | | | | 1 (16.7) | 1 (23.3) | | 4 (40.0) | 1 (3.3) | 2 (16.7) | | | |
| Netherlands (4.5) | 1 (4.4) | | | | | | 1 (15.6) | | 4 (33.3) | 3 (28.9) | 2 (15.6) | | 1 (2.2) | | |

| | 1 | 2 | 3 | 4 | 5 | 6 | 7 | 8 | 9 | 10 | 11 | 12 | 13 |
|---|---|---|---|---|---|---|---|---|---|---|---|---|---|
| Spain (12.0) | | | | | | | 1 (1.7) | 1 (0.8) | 5 (40.8) | 5 (24.8) | 3 (14.2) | 2 (17.5) | 1 (0.2) |
| Ireland (1.1) | | | | | | | | | | | 1 (100.0) | | |
| Greece (3.1) | | | | | | | | | | | 1 (6.4) | 8 (71.0) | 4 (22.6) |
| Portugal (3.2) | | | | | | | | | | | 1 (34.4) | 1 (18.8) | 3 (46.8) |
| EC (100.0) | 2 (0.6) | 2 (5.3) | 2 (1.2) | 5 (5.5) | 10 (6.2) | 18 (13.1) | 28 (16.1) | 33 (15.1) | 28 (14.9) | 13 (7.4) | 9 (6.0) | 12 (5.9) | 8 (2.5) |

*Source:* EC Commission (1990b).

*Table* 5.4   Regional income disparities within the European Community: ratios of the highest to the lowest income regions

|  | Within each country | Highest EC vs. lowest in each country | Proportion of each country's population in regions with ratios above the highest national (2.7) in the EC (%) |
|---|---|---|---|
| Luxembourg | – | 1.5 | 0 |
| West Germany | 2.4 | 2.4 | 0 |
| France | 2.2 | 2.4 | 0 |
| Denmark | 1.4 | 1.9 | 0 |
| UK | 2.0 | 2.3 | 0 |
| Italy | 2.3 | 3.1 | 15.2 |
| Belgium | 1.6 | 2.4 | 0 |
| Netherlands | 2.7 | 2.7 | 0 |
| Spain | 2.2 | 3.7 | 34.2 |
| Ireland | – | 2.8 | 100.0 |
| Greece | 1.7 | 4.6 | 93.6 |
| Portugal | 1.7 | 4.4 | 65.6 |
| *EC* | *4.6* | *4.6* | *12.9* |

*Source*: EC Commission (1990b).

socio-political conflicts and frictions that could lead to its disintegration, then income of about 13 per cent (equivalent to something like 43 million) of its existing inhabitants would have to be raised significantly to close the gap. With the exception of around 8.5 million Italians, all of them live in the four poorest EC countries.

It is possible that similar disparities existed also within 'The Club', though it is impossible either to prove or disprove this. The figures produced by Williamson (1965, pp. 54 and 68) give the following ratios for two countries: 2.8 for France in 1864 and 1.7 and 2.2 for Germany in 1900 and 1913 respectively. If correct, these ratios are comparable to those found in the 1980s *within* individual EC countries. But the sample is, unfortunately, too small to provide an adequate indication of whether regional differences in efficiency and income levels were greater, similar or smaller within 'The Club' than among EC countries. Hence, all that can be said confidently is that the latter *are* considerable when compared to the differences within member countries.

## INTERNATIONAL DISPARITIES IN ECONOMIC PERFORMANCE

The previous section analysed briefly the effect of long-term differences in economic performance of individual countries on their industrialisation, efficiency and income levels relative to those of other economies which were either members of the European Community or belonged to the classical gold standard. This section compares the extent of short- to medium-term convergence in a number of economic indicators for the same groups of countries. The comparison is relevant because 'convergence in economic performance' was singled out in the Treaty of Maastricht as the most important precondition for the viability of a monetary union of the kind to be formed by the Community.

Table 5.5 sets out a number of important indicators of economic performance for three groups of countries. The first of these, 'Classical Gold Standard 7' refers to the seven economies whose behaviour was analysed at some length in Chapter 2. The only difference is that this time Italy is treated as a member of 'The Club' for the simple reason that it was either formally or informally on the gold standard in each of the periods given in the table. 'EMS 8' includes the countries which have been members of the Community's exchange rate mechanism (ERM) throughout its existence: the Benelux countries, France, Germany, Italy and Ireland. 'EC 12', on the other hand, refers to these countries plus the remaining four members of the EC (Spain, Portugal, the UK and Greece) which have either joined the ERM recently or are still to do so.

The periods covered in Table 5.5 have been selected in a way which makes it possible to compare the extent of divergence in

*Table 5.5* Differences in economic performance among gold standard and EC countries
(coefficients of variation, %)

1. 1880–82, 1968–70     2. 1879–81, 1979–81     3. 1911–13, 1988–90

| | Classical gold standard 7 | | EMS 8 | | EC 12 | |
|---|---|---|---|---|---|---|
| | *Mean* | *Coefficient of variation* | *Mean* | *Coefficient of variation* | *Mean* | *Coefficient of variation* |
| **GDP** | | | | | | |
| 1 | 2.1 | 85.7 | (5.6) | (13.0) | (5.7) | (22.8) |
| 2 | 2.8 | 50.0 | 1.9 | 58.0 | 1.7 | 76.5 |
| 3 | (3.8) | (18.4) | 3.4 | 38.0 | 3.4 | 35.3 |
| First 12 years[a] | 2.2 | 50.0 | 2.4 | 21.0 | 2.4 | 21.0 |
| **Current balance of payments as % of GDP** | | | | | | |
| 1 | 0.7 | 300.0 | (–0.2) | (1 100.0) | (–0.3) | (733.3) |
| 2 | –0.3 | 1 033.3 | –3.3 | 142.4 | –2.8 | 146.4 |
| 3 | (0.7) | (528.6) | 1.0 | 190.0 | –0.5 | 520.0 |
| First 12 years[a] | 0.03 | 9 800.0 | –0.2 | 900.0 | –1.0 | 100.0 |
| **Consumer prices** | | | | | | |
| 1 | 1.1 | 100.0 | (4.5) | (46.7) | (4.4) | (40.9) |
| 2 | 1.7 | 82.4 | 10.4 | 50.0 | 13.0 | 46.2 |
| 3 | (1.9) | (57.9) | 3.6 | 38.9 | 5.8 | 24.9 |
| First 12 years[a] | –0.1 | 500.0 | 6.3 | 44.0 | 8.8 | 59.1 |
| **Unemployment** | | | | | | |
| 1 | | n.a. | (2.3) | (95.6) | (2.6) | (73.1) |
| 2 | | n.a. | 6.1 | 37.7 | 6.5 | 40.0 |
| 3 | | n.a. | 8.7 | 49.4 | 8.9 | 50.6 |
| First 12 years[a] | | n.a. | 8.4 | 43.4 | 8.9 | 43.7 |
| **Real wages** | | | | | | |
| 1 | 1.8 | 72.2 | (4.4) | (43.2) | (4.7) | (38.3) |
| 2 | 0.2 | 750.0 | 1.9 | 68.4 | 1.9 | 57.9 |
| 3 | (0.7) | (171.4) | 0.8 | 100.0 | 0.9 | 88.9 |
| First 12 years[a] | 1.8 | 22.0 | 1.0 | 70.0 | 1.1 | 63.6 |
| **Money supply** | | | | | | |
| 1 | 4.4 | 95.4 | (11.2) | (18.8) | (12.0) | (25.8) |
| 2 | 2.7 | 96.3 | 10.4 | 44.2 | 14.6 | 51.4 |
| 3 | (4.9) | (49.0) | 7.8 | 26.9 | 11.1 | 50.4 |
| First 12 years[a] | 3.4 | 52.9 | 9.2 | 23.0 | 12.9 | 46.5 |

| | Classical gold standard 7 | | EMS 8 | | EC 12 | |
|---|---|---|---|---|---|---|
| | *Mean* | *Coefficient of variation* | *Mean* | *Coefficient of variation* | *Mean* | *Coefficient of variation* |
| Interest rates | | | | | | |
| 1 | 4.0 | 10.0 | [b](6.4) | (21.9) | (6.3) | (28.6) |
| 2 | 3.9 | 7.7 | 13.3 | 19.6 | 14.0 | 17.1 |
| 3 | (4.9) | (10.2) | 9.6 | 19.8 | 11.2 | 26.8 |
| First 12 years[a] | 3.9 | 7.7 | 10.8 | 27.0 | 11.5 | 29.6 |
| 1 | | n.a. | [c](7.8) | (12.8) | (7.9) | (12.6) |
| 2 | | n.a. | 12.9 | 29.5 | 13.4 | 25.4 |
| 3 | | n.a. | 9.3 | 21.5 | 10.2 | 24.5 |
| First 12 years[a] | | n.a. | 11.5 | 24.0 | 12.2 | 22.9 |

[a]1880–91 and 1979–90.
[b]Nominal short-term rates.
[c]Nominal long-term rates.
*Sources*: Gold standard countries – see Table 2.1. EC countries – EC Commission (1990c).

economic performance of the gold standard and EMS countries both in the short to medium term and over a much longer period. In each case, the average figure for a country's indicator over a certain period is compared with averages of other countries in that group over the same period. The twelve-year time span has been chosen for no other reason than that this is how long the EMS has been in existence. The three-year periods are given partly to show the degree of similarity in the short-term economic behaviour of the countries concerned at comparable stages in the existence of the two monetary regimes and partly to observe changes, if any, in their economic convergence over a much longer time. Consequently, the table includes both the last three years of the classical gold standard (1911–13) as well as the last three years of the 'Bretton Woods System' (1968–70) when all EC countries were required to maintain fixed exchange rates.

Whatever the doubts that one may have about accuracy of the data presented in Table 5.5, the fact is that the comparisons produce results which are both interesting and consistent with what is known about the general characteristics of the two systems. For instance, it is clear that the degree of convergence in interest rates was appreciably greater under the gold standard than under the EMS. As one would expect, the difference is more pronounced when all EC countries are taken into account, though not much more so. The implication is that international financial integration was greater before 1914 – not exactly a surprising discovery. Although, as pointed in Chapter 1, many gold standard countries took steps to discourage outflows of gold – there were no exchange controls at the time, in contrast to their extensive use until recently by most members of the Community. The effect has been to reduce interest rate arbitrage in the EC to an extent that, as the gold standard experience suggests, would not have been possible without restrictions on capital flows.

On the other hand, there was a good deal more national *economic independence* within 'The Club' than in the EC, with ERM membership making apparently little difference. In other words, countries on the gold standard were less integrated and interdependent economically than members of the Community. Again, this is hardly surprising. Being less industrialised they were also much more self-sufficient. In addition, as shown in Chapter 3, many of them resorted to selective tariffs on imports, a policy instrument that is not available to EC countries on the most important part of their foreign trade: that with other members of the Community.

As a result of their greater economic self-sufficiency, countries adhering to the classical gold standard were able to sustain considerable variations in their growth rates in the short, medium and, as emphasised in Chapter 2, in the long term. This explains also the greater variations in their current balances of payments and money supply, neither of which would have been possible without the extraordinary flows of long-term international capital described in Chapter 3. The differences in national economic performance are also reflected in greater variations in inflation rates (around a much lower mean than in the Community) and in real wages.

Contrary to what might be expected, therefore, economic integration and interdependence within the Community appear to be already in many respects more extensive than under the gold standard, imposing a higher degree of convergence in economic performance than that which existed before the First World War. It is already difficult for an EC economy to stay out of step for long with developments in the rest of the Community, and this will become virtually impossible when the remaining barriers to trade and factor movements are removed. As usual in the case of economic integration, the constraint will be most apparent in the case of small and/or weaker economies whose performance will be largely determined by the objectives and policies of the dominant member country, or countries.

It is for this reason that the initial *levels* of efficiency and income are so important. Provided that they are similar in all members of a monetary union, the convergence in economic performance should not impose long-term social costs on any one of them. If two economies at comparable levels of productivity and income grow at the same rate their relative competitive position remains unchanged. That makes it relatively easy for them to pursue similar policies, ensuring that both their real and financial performance remain consistent with their membership of an international monetary union (Panić 1988).

It is, of course, precisely this very important condition that is difficult to satisfy if the initial efficiency and income levels are significantly different. In this case, similar rates of growth will impose increasing social costs on the weaker economy, as its productivity and income levels fall further and further behind those in the most affluent countries of the union. Close contact with the more advanced economies will encourage residents of the relatively poor country to copy their patterns of consumption. Consequently, foreign goods will be preferred to those produced domestically because of their superior quality and design. The effect of such a shift in a country's pattern of demand relative to its capacity to satisfy it is the familiar one of higher inflation, higher unemployment and – in the absence of a complete monetary union – larger current account deficits and, ultimately, the inability to sustain a particular exchange rate.

Moreover, under these conditions a relatively poor country finds it increasingly difficult to generate the level of domestic savings required to undertake the investment needed to correct its growing structural imbalance. Other things remaining the same, this means that the only way that it can stay in a monetary union is by reducing its rate of growth to a level which eliminates the problem of inflation, external deficits and exchange rate instability, but at the cost of higher unemployment. In theory, this is sustainable even in the long term. In practice, the interwar experience shows that no monetary union of sovereign nation states is likely to last long under these conditions.

The apparent need to impose a uniformity in economic performance on countries with significantly different underlying productivity and income levels has, therefore, policy implications for the European Community the importance of which cannot be emphasised too strongly. The data presented so far in this chapter show clearly that the EC has begun the process of creating a complete monetary union with appreciable disparities in efficiency and income levels; and these are bound to be exacerbated by a prolonged period of enforced convergence in the countries' economic performance – eventually making the planned monetary union unsustainable.

The only way to avoid such an outcome is for the more affluent countries and regions in the EC to pursue policies designed to raise efficiency and income levels in the rest of the Community. That, of course, requires reconciling for quite some time financial (inflation rates, basic balances of payments, interest rates) convergence with economic (growth of output and productivity) *divergence*. (For the extent to which the latter is needed in the Community, see EC Commission 1990b, especially 'Statistical Annexes', p. 6.) The problem is that the reconciliation is possible without severe and prolonged sacrifices in economic welfare only if it is supported by adequate international resource transfers – something that the EC countries have so far failed to achieve.

## MOBILITY OF LABOUR AND LONG-TERM CAPITAL WITHIN THE COMMUNITY

The most striking feature of factor movements within the Community is their size: they are small not only in absolute terms but also relative to factor flows between the twelve and the rest of the world. For example, the overall size of intra-EC migration can be judged from Tables 5.6 and 5.7 which show the proportion of foreigners (EC nationals and others) in the total and the working population of each member country at the beginning and end of the 1980s. (The only country missing from the tables is Italy for which comparable data are not available.)

As one would expect, foreigners are more prominent in the population and the labour force of the more affluent countries. But even there, the proportion of EC nationals is negligible, except in Luxembourg and Belgium – the two countries which host most of the Community's institutions. Moreover, there was apparently little change in this respect in the 1980s despite the arrival of the two new members (Portugal and Spain).

This observation is important because the Community has tried since its inception to promote free movement of labour between member states through a series of rules and regulations, all designed to outlaw discrimination against other EC nationals. The '1992' programme for the creation of a single internal market is intended, among other things, to create a completely unified labour market. Nevertheless, the effect on intra-EC labour mobility has remained modest – though the mobility has tended to vary, as under the classical gold standard, according to changes in the overall economic environment.

For instance, foreign labour assumed critical importance in

*Table* 5.6   Proportion of foreign nationals in total population (%)

| | 1983 | | | 1989 | | |
|---|---|---|---|---|---|---|
| | Total | EC nationals | Others | Total | EC nationals | Others |
| EC 12 | n.a. | n.a. | n.a. | 3.8 | 1.4 | 2.4 |
| EC 10[a] | 4.5 | 1.1 | 3.4 | 4.5 | 1.6 | 2.9 |
| Luxembourg | 26.1 | 15.7 | 10.4 | 26.6 | 24.7 | 1.9 |
| Belgium | 9.2 | 5.2 | 4.0 | 8.1 | 4.5 | 3.6 |
| West Germany | 7.5 | 1.9 | 5.7 | 7.7 | 2.3 | 5.4 |
| France | 7.5 | 0.9 | 6.6 | 7.2 | 2.5 | 4.7 |
| Netherlands | 3.9 | 1.0 | 2.9 | 4.0 | 1.2 | 2.8 |
| UK | 3.3 | 1.2 | 2.1 | 3.2 | 1.4 | 1.8 |
| Ireland | 2.4 | 1.9 | 0.5 | 2.2 | 1.8 | 0.4 |
| Denmark | 1.8 | 0.4 | 1.4 | 1.9 | 0.4 | 1.5 |
| Greece | 0.8 | 0.1 | 0.7 | 0.7 | 0.1 | 0.6 |
| Portugal | n.a. | n.a. | n.a. | 0.6 | 0.5 | 0.1 |
| Spain | n.a. | n.a. | n.a. | 0.3 | 0.1 | 0.2 |

[a]Excludes Spain and Portugal.
*Sources*: Eurostat (1985, 1991).

*Table* 5.7   Proportion of foreign workers in domestic labour force (%)

| | 1983 | | | 1989 | | |
|---|---|---|---|---|---|---|
| | Total | EC nationals | Others | Total | EC nationals | Others |
| EC 12 | n.a. | n.a. | n.a. | 5.0 | 2.1 | 2.9 |
| EC 10[a] | 5.0 | 1.4 | 3.6 | 6.0 | 2.5 | 3.5 |
| Luxembourg | 42.9 | 24.8 | 18.1 | 47.1 | 44.3 | 2.8 |
| West Germany | 8.9 | 2.5 | 6.4 | 8.9 | 3.1 | 5.8 |
| Belgium | 8.9 | 5.4 | 3.5 | 7.2 | 5.2 | 2.5 |
| France | 7.2 | 1.0 | 6.2 | 7.1 | 3.1 | 4.0 |
| Netherlands | 4.0 | 1.1 | 2.9 | 3.9 | 1.6 | 2.3 |
| UK | 4.0 | 1.6 | 2.4 | 3.8 | 1.8 | 2.0 |
| Ireland | 2.6 | 2.1 | 0.5 | 2.6 | 2.1 | 0.5 |
| Denmark | 1.7 | 0.6 | 1.1 | 2.0 | 0.6 | 1.4 |
| Portugal | n.a. | n.a. | n.a. | 0.7 | 0.1 | 0.6 |
| Greece | 0.7 | 0.1 | 0.6 | 0.6 | 0.1 | 0.5 |
| Spain | n.a. | n.a. | n.a. | 0.2 | 0.1 | 0.1 |

[a]Excludes Spain and Portugal.
*Sources*: See Table 5.6.

the receiving countries between 1960 and 1973 when they operated more or less continuously at the limits of their productive potential. Yet even in 1973 EC nationals accounted for only about 2 per cent of the total labour force in other Community countries (Molle 1990, p. 212). Among the relatively poorer countries which were to join the EC later, emigrants accounted for 19 per cent of the labour force in Portugal, 9 per cent in Greece and 4 per cent in Spain (ibid.).

The situation altered significantly after the first oil shock in 1973/4 which caused a sharp increase in unemployment even in the most successful economies. The result was a change in host countries' policies towards immigration, as they began actively to encourage repatriation and to impose restrictions on the entry of foreign nationals (cf. Lebon and Falchi 1980, Hammar 1985). Thousands of workers from the poorest countries returned home.

There is a very good reason why even '1992' and a significant improvement in the economic performance of EC countries are unlikely to reverse completely the past trends and, thus, turn labour mobility into a major factor in the adjustment process within the Community. The area which it covers is one of the most densely populated in the world. Hence, although various measures have been taken to ensure free movement of labour within the EC, the intention has never really been to generate large-scale migration of people within the area. As the Commission's recent report on regional policy points out, this is undesirable for the simple reason that it would create congestion and social problems on a scale that no country would be prepared to tolerate (EC Commission 1990b).

It would be completely unrealistic, therefore, to expect labour mobility to play even a remotely comparable role in the adjustment process within the EMU to that which it performed under the classical gold standard. With protection outlawed, this means that long-term capital flows have to assume an even more important role within the Community than they did before 1914. Yet this is an area in which EC performance has probably been even less impressive than in the case of labour mobility.

The paucity of relevant data makes capital flows one of the most difficult aspects of international transactions to analyse. The amount and quality of information provided about the volume and type of inward and outward investments vary a good deal from country to country. Moreover, the flows are normally recorded net of disinvestments, a method that can give a highly misleading picture of the actual volume of transactions involved. To make things worse, in a world of floating exchange rates annual changes in a particular type of international investment may reflect more short-term fluctuations in the value of one or more currencies than in that of actual capital flows. Finally, few countries have adequate information about the direction of their long-term capital flows – something that is particular relevance for the kind of analysis undertaken in this book.

For all these reasons, evidence concerning long-term capital flows within the EC has to be approached with some caution. Apart from the lack of statistical information, such data as are available tend to come predominantly from a relatively small number of countries (the UK, Germany, France, the Netherlands, Belgium and Luxembourg) which have traditionally featured prominently as both providers and recipients of international investment. The danger is, of course, that this may give a rather distorted view of the size and direction of the Community's long-term investments.

Nevertheless, even with these qualifications in mind, it is difficult to ignore the fact that all available data point in the same direction: at least until the early 1980s, intra-EC investments were far less important than those between the Community and the rest of the world (mainly the United States and, to a lesser extent, Japan). For instance, from the mid 1970s until the first half of the 1980s the proportion of EC investment going to non-member countries increased from about three-quarters to four-fifth of the total. In 1981–3 the highest proportion of extra-EC outflows was in portfolio investment (86.1 per cent), followed by direct investment (81.7 per cent) and other long-term capital (76.1 per cent) (Panić and Schioppa 1989, p. 181).

*Table 5.8*   EC foreign direct investment flows, 1975–83

| | Outflows | | | Inflows | | |
|---|---|---|---|---|---|---|
| | Total (billion ECU) | EC countries *(% of total)* | Others | Total (billion ECU) | EC countries *(% of total)* | Others |
| EC 12 | 108.5 | 28 | 72 | 79.1 | 39 | 61 |
| UK | 35.2 | 19 | 81 | 21.9 | 26 | 74 |
| West Germany | 23.7 | 29 | 71 | 8.7 | 40 | 60 |
| Netherlands | 20.8 | 35 | 65 | 9.1 | 25 | 75 |
| France | 16.4 | 33 | 67 | 11.9 | 51 | 49 |
| Belgium and Luxembourg | 5.3 | 57 | 43 | 8.5 | 53 | 47 |
| Italy | 4.6 | 20 | 80 | 5.8 | 48 | 52 |
| Spain | 1.2 | 17 | 83 | 6.7 | 49 | 51 |
| Denmark | 1.1 | 19 | 81 | 0.9 | 44 | 56 |
| Ireland | 0.2 | 50 | 50 | 3.7 | 35 | 65 |
| Greece | 0.0 | 0 | 0 | 1.2 | 25 | 75 |
| Portugal | 0.0 | 0 | 0 | 0.7 | 71 | 29 |

*Source*: Molle and Morsink (1991).

This conclusion is confirmed by what is probably the most comprehensive set of data concerning the direction of EC investments, produced by Molle and Morsink (1991) and summarised in Table 5.8. It covers the period 1975–83 and is confined to direct investment about which there is generally far more empirical evidence than about any other form of international capital flow. All the twelve current members of the Community are included, even though Greece did not join the EC until 1981 and Portugal and Spain until 1986.

Taking the period as a whole, 60 per cent of the total inflows into the twelve economies came from third countries (mainly the United States) which also absorbed 70 per cent of EC direct outward investment (the largest share going to the US). Moreover, Denmark apart, it is economically the most advanced members that accounted for the bulk of the Community's direct investment, both as investors and borrowers. Portugal, Greece and Ireland received only around 7 per cent of the inflows – with most of them coming, except in the case of

*Table* 5.9　Average annual inflows of foreign direct investment as a proportion of gross domestic fixed capital formation (%)

|  | 1980–2 | 1985–7 |
|---|---|---|
| UK | 8.2 | 8.8 |
| Netherlands | 5.8 | 8.4 |
| Greece | 6.3 | 7.4 |
| Spain | 4.1 | 7.3 |
| Belgium and Luxembourg | 7.6 | 6.6 |
| Portugal | 2.1 | 4.1 |
| France | 1.8 | 2.7 |
| Ireland | 4.4 | 1.8 |
| Italy | 0.8 | 1.3 |
| Denmark | 1.1 | 0.8 |
| West Germany | 0.3 | 0.6 |
| *Mean*: | | |
| European Community | 3.9 | 4.5 |
| All developed market economies | 2.9 | 3.4 |

*Source*: United Nations (1991, pp. 7–8).

Portugal, from outside the Community. Spain, on the other hand, attracted more foreign direct investment than Italy, with about half of it provided by EC countries.

On the whole, the contribution made by foreign direct investment to the gross fixed capital formation in individual countries (Table 5.9) is rather modest – especially in the less advanced member countries – compared to the assistance which foreign investment provided to the less industrialised members of 'The Club' under the classical gold standard (see Chapter 3). Furthermore, unlike in the period before 1914, four of the six countries in which the contribution of foreign direct investment is most prominent also happen to enjoy some of the highest efficiency and income levels within the EC. Lastly, judging by the data in Table 5.8, most of these contributions were made by investors outside the Community.

What is not clear from available evidence is whether the situation has changed significantly since the early 1980s and, if so, to what extent. It can be seen from Table 5.9 that the importance of foreign direct investment in gross fixed capital formation has increased since then in all the new member states – Greece, Spain and Portugal – especially the last two. (See also United Nations 1990.) They seem, therefore, to have benefited from the sizeable expansion in intra-EC direct investment in the 1980s, caused by the prospect of a single European market (cf. United Nations 1991). However, the existing evidence is much less helpful in deciding whether EC firms have played a more prominent role in these intra-EC investments than their US and Japanese counterparts, or whether the unusually high levels of intra-EC investments, brought about by cross-border rationalisation of company activities, will continue into the 1990s. There is some evidence that large transnationals, which account for most international direct investment, had already by the end of the 1980s completed a considerable part of their restructuring in response to '1992' (United Nations 1990, p. 20).

It is even less clear whether developments similar to those observed in the case of direct investment in the 1980s also apply to portfolio and other long-term capital, as the relevant data are not available. What is known is that the segmentation of EC stock markets, through national regulations and exchange controls, prevented their integration at least until the early 1980s (Stonham 1982). Not surprisingly, as already mentioned, most of these markets had much closer links with those in third countries, notably the United States, than with similar markets in the Community. However, there is some evidence that EC capital markets have become much more integrated since then (Corner and Tonks 1987), as a result of deliberate efforts by national authorities (Stonham 1987). At the same time, what this evidence suggests is that portfolio and other long-term capital are moving more freely now between the largest and most advanced economies in the Community, rather than that they are playing a more prominent role in financing a greater transfer of resources from them to the less affluent countries and regions of the EC.

CONCLUSION AND ITS POLICY IMPLICATIONS

Given the problems normally associated with comparing historical data, especially those concerning worlds as different as Europe in the 1990s and Europe before the First World War, the best that can be said about the preceding analysis is that *national* disparities in efficiency and income levels appear to be about the same in the European Community as they were among the countries which participated in the international monetary union throughout the gold standard period.

The implications, as pointed out earlier, is that existing differences within the EC need not be unsustainable, in the sense of threatening not just the success but the very existence of a European monetary union. However, given the fact that members of the Community will have much less independence in conducting the policies needed to solve their national economic problems than had the individual nation states on the classical gold standard, the degree of international cooperation and coordination of policies will now need to be that much greater. Limited economic sovereignty also implies the necessity of generating a substantial transfer of resources – private *and* official – within the EC. This will obviously need to be on a smaller scale than between members of 'The Club', for the simple reason that no EC country has to undertake urbanisation and the development of infrastructure on the scale required in many countries before 1914. Nevertheless, given the existing disparities in the Community, the transfers will have to be considerable. The reason for this is that, as emphasised throughout this book, the gold standard was largely sustained by massive international movements of people and capital, chiefly between members of 'The Club'.

Although encouraged by national policies, the unprecedented movements of capital and labour between 1880 and 1914 were induced chiefly by the complementarity of resource endowments, especially among the countries which stayed on the gold standard throughout its existence. By contrast, resource endowments within the EC are much more competitive than complementary; and the scope for labour migration between EC countries is far more limited because of the high population density, especially in the most prosperous areas. In addition, the demand for a high level of employment, continuous improvements in the standard of living and a more equitable distribution of income is greater now than before 1914. This means that contemporary governments have to pay much more attention to these objectives than did their predecessors before the First World War. The further the Community advances towards creating an economic union which limits the ability of nation states to achieve these goals independently the more it will have to develop the means for doing so collectively. That much seems to be recognised in the Single European Act and attempts by the Commission to formulate more effective EC regional policies as well as a social charter.

It is less clear that there is much awareness of the potentially large-scale resource transfers that a European monetary union is likely to require – given the existing disparities in national efficiency and income levels and the fact that the degree of complementarity among EC countries is smaller than it was among the gold standard countries. The resources devoted by the Community to the development of its poorest countries and regions have been paltry compared to their needs; and the planned increases are on nowhere near the scale required to reduce the gap between them and the most advanced countries and regions to a level comparable to that either within the latter or within a large nation state such as the United States (cf. Kowalski 1989). Even the EC Commission (1990b, p. vi) recognises that resource transfers through the Structural Fund will have only a 'limited . . . impact on income disparities . . .'. Yet, judging by the gold standard experience, it is the ability to generate and maintain an adequate transfer of resources within it that will determine the long-term survival of a European monetary and economic union.

The reason for this, emphasised in the earlier chapters, is that individual countries adopted the classical gold standard and stayed on it only so long as it did not interfere with their national economic objectives. Thus, 'Sweden, like almost all countries before and after 1914, observed the gold standard orthodoxy [i.e. the membership of an international monetary union] when it made no difference to the domestic economy, but abandoned it [in 1931] as soon as it began to bind. . . . Sweden stayed on the gold standard peacefully because she grew rapidly, and not vice versa' (Lindert 1984, pp. 402–3). Had the country been less able to attract foreign investment on the scale required to sustain rapid growth, Sweden might have shared Italy's experience in discovering that 'the gold standard was not a sufficient condition for stability. Politicians had no difficulties in throwing off the straightjacket of the gold standard [in the early 1890s] when it stood in the way of financing large budget deficits' (Fratianni and Spinelli 1984, p. 417).

These quotations refer to differences in the experience and responses of two relatively less industrialised countries during the gold standard period. However, it is not only a country with a relatively weak economy, like Italy in the nineteenth century, that may decide to leave a monetary union because it finds the cost of membership unacceptably high. A similar response can be expected also from the strongest members of such a union if they are required to make what they regard as an unreasonably large contribution towards sustaining it.

Slovenia, the wealthiest republic in Yugoslavia, and the first to leave the federation, provides a timely reminder of this possibility. As one might expect from a people as ingenious as the Slovenes, their declaration of independence was wrapped up in the kind of rhetoric likely to appeal to West European public opinion: 'freedom', 'democracy' and 'the right of a small nation to self-determination'. In fact, the real reason was much more prosaic: the long-standing resentment of the Slovenes that, as they saw it, their own economic welfare had suffered irreparably because of the contribution which they had to make towards helping much poorer southern republics of Yugoslavia. Unable to persuade other members of the federation to agree to a major reduction in their fiscal contribution, they exploited the earliest opportunity presented by dramatic changes in Eastern Europe to leave, with EC approval, the Yugoslav economic, monetary and political union.

It would no doubt be unfair to accuse the Germans of giving such a strong support to Slovenia's quest for independence in order to set a precedent that they themselves might wish to follow at some future date. But it would equally be unwise to ignore the fact that this is precisely what Germany or some other wealthy member (or members) of the proposed European monetary and economic union might do if the cost of membership proved to be unacceptable to the majority of its population. Consequently, a failure by the architects of the EC or similar international monetary unions to take this factor into account might yet turn 'the Slovenia syndrome' into a common, widely recognised phenomenon rather than something confined to a handful of warring Slavs.

It is for all these reasons that the optimum solution in Europe seems to lie in the creation of a two-tier monetary union: a *complete union* comprising economies with the highest, comparable efficiency and income levels; and a *quasi union* between them and other European countries that would like to join a monetary union but could remain in the top tier only with the help of sizeable transfers of resources from other members over many years.

Such a two-tier structure would also make it possible for different policy requirements to be applied within and between the two groups: gradual harmonisation within the top tier and a clear policy differentiation between these policies and those to be followed by members of the quasi monetary union who are not in the top tier. The latter could also be allowed a much greater diversity of national policies, enabling each country to select the package of economic measures most suitable to its own specific problems as well as the length of time over which it is to be implemented. Once an economy reaches efficiency and income levels comparable to those of countries in the top tier, it could join them as this would not impose costs in economic welfare that either its own population or those of its partners might find unacceptable.

Which of the existing EC members ought to join which tier is obviously something that should be determined pragmatically, according to the volume of resource transfers that would be required to ensure their lasting membership and the willingness of the most affluent members of the Community to provide them. Moreover, on the basis of this criterion, it would be relatively easy for the complete union to absorb eventually the remaining Scandinavian countries, Switzerland and Austria should they wish to join it. The quasi monetary union, on the other hand, could be expanded gradually to include East European economies as they become ready to sustain the rigours of an international monetary union.

Although a two-tier approach represents the only way to create a lasting European monetary union, it is bound to be resented strongly for political reasons – particularly by the countries whose economies are not strong enough to cope with the pace of change and the discipline of policy synchronisation demanded of those in the top tier. Considerations of national prestige and the pressure from commercial interests confident that they would do well within a complete union, combined with the hope of poorer regions that they would receive a larger slice of foreign aid if their country joined the top tier – all add up to a powerful combination that many governments might find difficult to resist. Nevertheless, given the limited volume of resource transfers that the Community can realistically be expected to mobilise, their long-term chances of remaining in the complete union are likely to be even smaller than those of the countries that found the much less demanding arrangements under the classical gold standard too costly.

In conclusion, judging by the experience of the much less complex world which existed before 1914, members of the European Community – present and future – have the following two options: either to agree on policies and resource transfers that harmonise their efficiency and income *levels* and, thus, their long-term economic performance, or to differentiate their economic institutional frameworks and policies until they are able and willing to adopt the first option. A complete monetary union is compatible with the first but not with the second alternative. Indeed, some European countries may find for quite some time that even the acceptance of the rules of a quasi monetary union imposes on them welfare costs which are unacceptably high. It would be much less costly in the long term to all concerned, therefore, if these differences were fully recognised and allowed to shape Europe's institutional changes *before* rather than after the creation of a complete monetary union.

# References

BAIROCH, P. (1976) *Commerce Extérieur et Développement Economique de l'Europe au XIX Siècle* (Paris: Ecole des Hautes Etudes en Sciences Sociales).

BAIROCH, P. (1981) 'The Main Trends in National Economic Disparities Since the Industrial Revolution', in P. Bairoch and M. Levy-Leboyer (eds): *Disparities in Economic Development Since the Industrial Revolution* (London: Macmillan).

BAIROCH, P. (1982) 'International Industrialisation Levels from 1750 to 1980', *Journal of European Economic History* (Spring).

BAIROCH, P. (1989a) 'The Paradoxes of Economic History', *European Economic Review* (March).

BAIROCH, P. (1989b) 'European Trade Policy, 1815–1914', in P. Mathias and S. Pollard (1989).

Bank of England (1984) 'The Variability of Exchange Rates – Measurement and Effect', *Bank of England Quarterly Bulletin* (September).

BLOOMFIELD, A. I. (1959) *Monetary Policy Under the International Gold Standard: 1880–1914* (New York: Federal Reserve Bank of New York).

BLOOMFIELD, A. I. (1963) 'Short-Term Capital Movements Under the Pre-1914 Gold Standard', *Princeton Studies in International Finance* (Princeton: Princeton University Press).

BLOOMFIELD, A. I. (1968) 'Patterns of Fluctuations in International Investment Before 1914', *Princeton Studies in International Finance* (Princeton: Princeton University Press).

BOLTHO, A. (1989) 'Did Policy Activism Work?', *European Economic Review* (December).

BURGENMEIER, B. and MUCCHIELLI, J. L. (eds) (1991) *Multinationals and Europe 1992* (London: Routledge).

CAIRNCROSS, A. K. (1953) *Home and Foreign Investment, 1870–1913* (Cambridge: Cambridge University Press).

CASSEL, G. (1935) *The Downfall of the Gold Standard* (Oxford: Clarendon Press).

CHANDLER, A. D. (1977) *The Visible Hand: The Managerial Revolution in American Business* (Cambridge, Mass.: The Belknap Press of the Harvard University Press).

CHANDLER, A. D. (1986) 'The Evolution of Modern Global Competition', in M. E. Porter (ed.): *Competition in Global Industries* (Boston: Harvard Business School Press).

COHEN, J. S. (1967) 'Financing Industrialisation in Italy, 1894–1914: the Partial Transformation of a Late-Comer', *Journal of Economic History* (September).

COOPER, R. N. (1982) 'The Gold Standard: Historical Facts and Future Prospects', *Brooking Papers on Economic Activity* (No. 1).

161

CORDEN, W. M. (1972) 'Monetary Integration', *Princeton Essays in International Finance* (Princeton: Princeton University Press).

CORNER, D. C. and TONKS, I. (1987) 'The Impact of the Internationalisation of World Stock Markets on the Integration of EC Securities Markets', in M. Macmillan, D. G. Mayer and P. van Veen (eds): *European Integration and Industry* (Tilburg: Tilburg University Press).

DAVIS, L. E. and HUTTENBACK, R. A. (1988) *Mammon and the Pursuit of Empire – the Economics of British Imperialism* (Cambridge: Cambridge University Press).

DELORS COMMITTEE (1989) *Report on Economic and Monetary Union in the European Community* (Luxembourg: Office for Official Publications of the EC).

DOMAR, E. D. (1957) *Essays in the Theory of Economic Growth* (New York: Oxford University Press).

DUNNING, J. H. (1988) 'Changes in the Level and Structure of International Production: the Last 100 Years', in J. H. Dunning: *Explaining International Production* (London: Unwin Hyman).

EC COMMISSION (1977) *Report of the Study Group on the Role of the Public Finance in European Integration*, 2 vols (Brussels).

EC COMMISSION (1990a) 'One Market, One Money: An Evaluation of the Potential Benefits and Costs of Forming an Economic and Monetary Union', *European Economy* (October).

EC COMMISSION (1990b) *The Regions in the 1990s* (Brussels: mimeo).

EC COMMISSION (1990c) 'Statistical Annex', *European Economy* (December).

EDELSTEIN, M. (1982) *Overseas Investment in the Age of British Imperialism: the United Kingdom, 1850–1914* (New York: Columbia University Press).

EICHENGREEN, B. (ed.) (1985) *The Gold Standard in Theory and History* (London: Methuen).

EICHENGREEN, B. (1992) *Golden Fetters – the Gold Standard and the Great Depression, 1919–1939* (New York: Oxford University Press).

Eurostat (1985) *Labour Force Sample Survey, 1983* (Luxembourg).

Eurostat (1991) *Labour Force Survey, 1989* (Luxembourg).

FEINSTEIN, C. (1990) 'What Really Happened to Real Wages? Trends in Wages, Prices and Productivity in the United Kingdom, 1880–1913', *Economic History Review* (August).

FISHLOW, A. (1985) 'Lessons from the Past: Capital Markets During the 19th Century and the Interwar Period', *International Organisation* (Summer).

FLEETWOOD, E. E. (1947) *Sweden's Capital Imports and Exports* (Geneva: Institut Universitaire des Hautes Etudes Internationales).

FLEMING, J. M. (1971) 'On Exchange Rate Unification', *Economic Journal* (September).

FORD, A. G. (1962) *The Gold Standard 1880–1914: Britain and Argentina* (Oxford: Clarendon Press).

FORD, A. G. (1989) 'International Financial Policy and the Gold Standard, 1870–1914', in P. Mathias and S. Pollard (1989).

FOREMAN-PECK, J. (1983) *A History of the World Economy – Inter-*

*national Economic Relations Since* 1850 (Brighton: Wheatsheaf Books).
FRATIANNI, M. and SPINELLI, F. (1984) 'Italy in the Gold Standard Period, 1861–1914', in M. D. Bordo and A. J. Schwartz (eds): *A Retrospective on the Classical Gold Standard, 1821–1931* (Chicago: University of Chicago Press).
FRENKEL, J. A. and JOHNSON, H. G. (eds) (1976) *The Monetary Approach to the Balance of Payments* (London: Allen & Unwin).
FRIEDMAN, M. (1990) 'Bimetallism Revisited', *Journal of Economic Perspectives* (Fall).
GILLE, B. (1973) 'Banking and Industrialisation in Europe, 1730–1914', in C. M. Cipolla (ed.): *The Fontana Economic History of Europe. Vol. 3. The Industrial Revolution* (Glasgow: Fontana/Collins).
GORDON, R. J. (1982) 'Why US Wage and Employment Behaviour Differs from that in Britain and Japan', *Economic Journal* (March).
GOSCHEN, G. J. ([1861] 1890) *The Theory of the Foreign Exchange* (London: Effingham Wilson).
GOULD, J. D. (1979) 'European Inter-continental Emigration, 1815–1914 – Patterns and Causes', *Journal of European Economic History* (Winter).
GREEN, A. and URQUHART, M. C. (1976) 'Factor and Commodity Flows in the International Economy of 1870–1914: A Multi-Country View', *Journal of Economic History* (March).
GUISINGER, S. E. and Associates (1985) *Investment Incentives and Performance Requirements* (New York: Praeger).
HABERLER, G. (1970) 'The International Monetary System: Some Recent Developments and Discussions', in G. N. Halm (ed.): *Approaches to Greater Flexibility of Exchange Rates* (Princeton: Princeton University Press).
HAMMAR, T. (1985) *European Immigration Policy* (Cambridge: Cambridge University Press).
HARROD, R. F. (1948) *Towards a Dynamic Economics* (London: Macmillan).
HARTLAND, P. (1949) 'Interregional Payments Compared with International Payments', *Quarterly Journal of Economics* (August).
HOOVER, E. D. (1960) 'Retail Prices After 1850', in NBER: *Trends in the American Economy in the Nineteenth Century* (Princeton: Princeton University Press).
HUME, D. ([1752] 1985) 'On the Balance of Trade', in B. Eichengreen (1985).
IMF (1984) 'The Exchange Rate System – Lessons of the Past and Options for the Future', *Occasional Paper No. 30* (Washington, D. C.).
INGRAM, J. C. (1957) 'Growth and Canada's Balance of Payments', *American Economic Review* (March).
INGRAM, J. C. (1973) 'The Case for European Monetary Integration', *Princeton Essays in International Finance* (Princeton: Princeton University Press).
ISARD, P. (1977) 'How Far Can We Push the Law of One Price?', *American Economic Review* (December).
JOHNSON, H. G. (1972) 'The Case for Flexible Exchange Rates, 1969', in

H. G. Johnson: *Further Essays in Monetary Economics* (Cambridge, Mass.: Harvard University Press).

JONUNG, L. (1984) 'Swedish Experience Under the Classical Gold Standard, 1873–1914', in M. D. Bordo and A. J. Schwartz (eds): *A Retrospective on the Classical Gold Standard, 1821–1931* (Chicago: University of Chicago Press).

JORBERG, L. (1973) 'The Nordic Countries 1850–1914', in C. M. Cipolla (ed.): *The Fontana Economic History of Europe. Vol. 4. The Emergence of Industrial Societies – Part Two* (Glasgow: Fontana/Collins).

KEMP, T. (1969) *Industrialisation in Nineteenth-Century Europe* (London: Longmans).

KENEN, P. B. (1969) 'The Theory of Optimum Currency Areas: an Ecclectic View', in R. A. Mundell and A. K. Swoboda (eds): *Monetary Problems in the International Economy* (Chicago: University of Chicago Press).

KENWOOD, A. G. and LOUGHEED, A. L. (1983) *The Growth of the International Economy 1820–1980* (London: Allen & Unwin).

KEYNES, J. M. ([1930] 1971) *A Treatise on Money – The Applied Theory of Money* (London: Macmillan).

KINDLEBERGER, C. P. (1973) *The World in Depression, 1929–1939* (London: Allen Lane).

KINDLEBERGER, C. P. (1978) *Manias, Panics and Crashes: A History of Financial Crises* (New York: Basic Books).

KINDLEBERGER, C. P. (1984) *A Financial History of Europe* (London: Allen & Unwin).

KINDLEBERGER, C. P. (1985) 'The Cyclical Patterns of Long-Term Lending', in C. P. Kindleberger: *Keynesianism vs. Monetarism and Other Essays in Financial History* (London: Allen & Unwin).

KOWALSKI, L. (1989) 'Major Current and Future Regional Issues in the Enlarged Community', in L. Albrechts, F. Moulaert, P. Roberts and E. Swyngedouw (eds): *Regional Policy at the Crossroads – European Perspectives* (London: Jessica Kingsley).

KRAVIS, I. B. and LIPSEY, R. E. (1971) *Price Competitiveness in World Trade* (New York: National Bureau of Economic Research).

KRAVIS, I. B. and LIPSEY, R. E. (1978) 'Price Behaviour in the Light of Balance of Payments Theories', *Journal of International Economics* (May).

KRUGMAN, P. R. (ed.) (1986) *Strategic Trade Policy and the New International Economics* (Cambridge, Mass.: MIT Press).

KUZNETS, S. (1966) *Modern Economic Growth* (New Haven: Yale University Press.)

LEAGUE OF NATIONS (1927) *Tariff Level Indices* (Geneva).

LEBON, A. and FALCHI, G. (1980) 'New Developments in Intra-European Migration Since 1974', *International Migration Review* (Winter).

LETWIN, W. (1989) 'American Economic Policy, 1865–1939', in P. Mathias and S. Pollard (1989).

LEWIS, C. (1938) *America's Stake in International Investments* (Washington, D.C.: Brookings Institution).

LEWIS, W. A. (1952) 'World Production, Prices and Trade, 1870–1960', *Manchester School*, (May).

LEWIS, W. A. (1978a) *Growth and Fluctuations 1870–1913* (London: Allen & Unwin).

LEWIS, W. A. (1978b) *The Evolution of the International Economic Order* (Princeton: Princeton University Press).

LINDERT, P. H. (1969) 'Key Currencies and Gold 1900–1913', *Princeton Studies in International Finance* (Princeton: Princeton University Press).

LINDERT, P. H. (1984) 'Comments', in M. D. Bordo and A. J. Schwartz (eds): *A Retrospective on the Classical Gold Standard, 1821–1931* (Chicago: University of Chicago Press).

McCLOSKEY, D. N. and ZECHER, J. R. (1976) 'How the Gold Standard Worked, 1880–1913', in J. A. Frenkel and H. G. Johnson (1976).

McCLOSKEY, D. N. and ZECHER, J. R. (1984) 'The Success of Purchasing-Power Parity: Historical Evidence and Its Implications for Macroeconomics', in M. D. Bordo and A. J. Schwartz (eds): *A Retrospective on the Classical Gold Standard*, 1821–1931 (Chicago: University of Chicago Press).

McKINNON, R. I. (1963) 'Optimum Currency Areas', *American Economic Review* (September).

McKINNON, R. I. (1964) 'Foreign Exchange Constraints in Economic Development and Efficient Aid Allocation', *Economic Journal* (June).

MADDISON, A. (1962) 'Growth and Fluctuations in the World Economy, 1870–1960', *Banca Nazionale del Lavoro Quarterly Review* (June).

MADDISON, A. (1982) *Phases of Capitalist Development* (Oxford: Oxford University Press).

MADDISON, A. (1989) *The World Economy in the 20th Century* (Paris: OECD).

MATHIAS, P. and POLLARD, S. (eds) (1989) *The Cambridge Economic History of Europe. Vol. VIII. The Industrial Economies: The Development of Economic and Social Policies* (Cambridge: Cambridge University Press).

MEADE, J. E. (1957) 'The Balance of Payments Problem in a Free Trade Area', *Economic Journal* (September).

MILL, J. S. ([1848] 1965) *Principles of Political Economy*, J. M. Robson (ed.) (London: Routledge & Keegan Paul).

MILWARD, A. and SAUL, S. B. (1977) *The Development of the Economies of Continental Europe, 1850–1914* (London: Allen & Unwin).

MITCHELL, B. R. (1975) *European Historical Statistics, 1750–1970* (London: Macmillan).

MITCHELL, B. R. (1983) *International Historical Statistics: The Americas and Australasia* (London: Macmillan).

MOGGRIDGE, D. (1972) *British Monetary Policy, 1924–1931* (Cambridge: Cambridge University Press).

MOLLE, W. (1990) *The Economics of European Integration* (Aldershot: Dartmouth).

MOLLE, W. and MORSINK, R. (1991) 'Intra-European Direct Investment', in B. Burgenmeier and J. L. Mucchielli (1991).

MORGENSTERN, O. (1959) *International Financial Transactions and Business Cycles* (Princeton: Princeton University Press).

MUNDELL, R. A. (1961) 'A Theory of Optimum Currency Areas', *American Economic Review* (September).

MYRDAL, G. (1957) *Economic Theory and Underdeveloped Regions* (London: Duckworth).

NURKSE, R. (1944) *International Currency Experience: Lessons of the Interwar Period* (Geneva: League of Nations).

PANIĆ, M. (1976) 'The Inevitable Inflation' *Lloyds Bank Review* (July).

PANIĆ, M. (1978) 'The Origin of Increasing Inflationary Tendencies in Contemporary Society', in F. Hirsch and J. H. Goldthorpe (eds): *The Political Economy of Inflation* (London: Martin Robertson).

PANIĆ, M. (1982) 'International Direct Investment in Conditions of Structural Disequilibrium – UK Experience Since the 1960s', in J. Black and J. H. Dunning (eds): *International Capital Movements* (London: Macmillan).

PANIĆ, M. (1988) *National Management of the International Economy* (London: Macmillan and New York: St Martin's Press).

PANIĆ, M. (1990) 'Economic Development and Trade Policy', *DAE Working Paper 9006* (Cambridge: Department of Applied Economics, University of Cambridge).

PANIĆ, M. (1991) 'The Impact of Multinationals on National Economic Policies', in B. Burgenmeier and J. L. Mucchielli (1991).

PANIĆ, M. and SCHIOPPA, C. (1989) 'Europe's Long-Term Capital Flows Since 1971', in I. Gordon and A. P. Thirlwall (eds): *European Factor Mobility – Trends and Consequences* (London: Macmillan).

PHELPS BROWN, E. H. and BROWNE, M. H. (1968) *A Century of Pay* (London: Macmillan).

POHL, K. O. (1990) 'Prospects of the European Monetary Union', in K. O. Pohl *et al.*: *Britain and EMU* (London: London School of Economics).

RIIS, C. and THONSTAD, T. (1989) 'A Counterfactual Study of Economic Impact of Norwegian Emigration and Capital Imports', in I. Gordon and A. P. Thirlwall (eds): *European Factor Mobility – Trends and Consequences* (London: Macmillan).

ROSENSTEIN-RODAN, P. N. (1961) 'International Aid for Underdeveloped Countries', *Review of Economics and Statistics* (May).

ROSTOW, W. W. (1978) *The World Economy: History and Prospects* (London: Macmillan).

ROSTOW, W. W. (1980) *Why The Poor Get Richer and the Rich Slow Down* (London: Macmillan).

SACHS, J. (1980) 'The Changing Cyclical Behaviour of Wages and Prices: 1890–1976', *American Economic Review* (March).

SALTER, W. E. G. (1966) *Productivity and Technical Change*, 2nd edn (Cambridge: Cambridge University Press).

SANDBERG, L. (1979) 'The Case of the Impoverished Sophisticate: Human Capital and Swedish Growth Before World War I', *Journal of Economic History* (March).

SCITOVSKY, T. (1958) *Economic Theory and Western European Integration* (London: Allen & Unwin).

SEGAL, H. H. and SIMON, M. (1961) 'British Foreign Capital Issues, 1865–94', *Journal of Economic History* (December).

SEN, G. (1984) *The Military Origins of Industrialisation and International Trade Rivalry* (London: Frances Pinter).

SIMON, M. (1967) 'The Pattern of New British Foreign Investment, 1865–1914', in J. H. Adler (ed.): *Capital Movements and Economic Development* (London: Macmillan).

STONHAM, P. (1982) *Major Stock Markets of Europe* (Aldershot: Gower).

STONHAM, P. (1987) *Global Stock Market Reforms* (Aldershot: Gower).

SUMMERS, R. and HESTON, A. (1988) 'A New Set of International Comparisons of Real Products and Prices: Estimates for 130 Countries, 1950–1985', *Review of Income and Wealth* (March).

SUMMERS, R. and HESTON, A. (1991) 'The Pen World Table (Mark 5): An Expanded Set of International Comparisons, 1950–1988', *Quarterly Journal of Economics* (May).

SUNDSTROM, W. A. (1990) 'Was There a Golden Age of Flexible Wages? Evidence from Ohio Manufacturing, 1892–1910', *Journal of Economic History* (June).

SUPPLE, B. (1973) 'The State and the Industrial Revolution 1700–1914', in C. M. Cipolla (ed.): *Fontana Economic History of Europe. Vol. 3. The Industrial Revolution* (Glasgow: Fontana/Collins).

TAUSSIG, F. W. (1927) *International Trade* (New York: Macmillan).

THOMAS, B. (1973) *Migration and Economic Growth*, 2nd edn (Cambridge: Cambridge University Press).

THORNTON, H. ([1802] 1939) *An Inquiry into the Nature and Effects of the Paper Credit of Great Britain* (London: Allen & Unwin).

TINBERGEN, J. (1951) *Business Cycles in the United Kingdom 1870–1914* (Amsterdam: North-Holland).

TRIFFIN, R. (1964) 'The Evolution of the International Monetary System: Historical Reappraisal and Future Perspectives', *Princeton Studies in International Finance* (Princeton: Princeton University Press).

TRIFFIN, R. (1968) *Our International Monetary System: Yesterday, Today and Tomorrow* (New York: Random House).

UNITED NATIONS (1979) *Trends and Characteristics of International Migration Since 1950* (New York: United Nations).

UNITED NATIONS (1990) 'Regional Economic Integration and Transnational Corporations in the 1990s: Europe 1992, North America, and Developing Countries', *UNCTC Current Studies, Series A, No. 15* (New York: UN Centre on Transnational Corporations).

UNITED NATIONS (1991) *World Investment Report 1991 – The Triad in Foreign Direct Investment* (New York).

VINER, J. (1924) *Canada's Balance of International Indebtedness, 1900–1913* (Cambridge, Mass.: Harvard University Press).

VINER, J. (1937) *Studies in the Theory of International Trade* (London: Allen & Unwin).

WHALE, P. B. (1937) 'The Working of the Prewar Gold Standard', *Economica* (February).

WHITE, H. D. (1933) *The French International Accounts, 1880–1913* (Cambridge, Mass.: Harvard University Press).

WICKSELL, K. ([1898] 1936) *Interest and Prices* (London: Macmillan).

WILKINS, M. (1989) *The History of Foreign Investment in the United States to 1914* (Cambridge, Mass.: Harvard University Press).

WILLIAMS, J. H. (1920) *Argentine International Trade Under Incontrovertible Paper Money 1880–1900* (Cambridge, Mass.: Harvard University Press).

WILLIAMSON, J. G. (1965) 'Regional Inequality and the Process of National Development – A Description of the Patterns', *Economic Development and Cultural Change* (July).

WOODRUFF, W. (1982) *Impact of Western Man* (Washington, DC: University Press of America).

WORLD BANK (1985) *World Development Report* (Washington, DC).

WOYTINSKY, W. S. and WOYTINSKY, E. S. (1955) *World Commerce and Governments – Trends and Outlook* (New York: Twentieth Century Fund).

YEAGER, L. B. (1984) 'The Image of the Gold Standard', in M. D. Bordo and A. J. Schwartz (eds): *A Retrospective on the Classical Gold Standard, 1821–1931* (Chicago: University of Chicago Press).

# Index

*Index*